STORYTELLING
For The FUN Of It
A Handbook for Children

Vivian Dubrovin

Illustrated By Bobbi Shupe

STORYCRAFT
PUBLISHING

Masonville, CO 80541

Storycraft books are available at special discount for bulk purchases
for workshops, classes, promotions, or fund raising. Special editions
or book excerpts can also be created. For details contact:
Sales Director, Storycraft Publishing, P.O. Box 205, Masonville, CO 80541

Storycraft Publishing
P.O. Box 205
Masonville, CO 80541

Printed in the United States of America

Publisher's Cataloging-in-Publication
(Provided by Quality Books, Inc.)

Dubrovin, Vivian.
    Storytelling for the fun of it : a handbook for children /
Vivian Dubrovin ; illustrated by Bobbi Shupe. -- Rev. ed.
    p. cm.
    Includes bibliographical references and index.
    SUMMARY: Introduces young people (ages 9-12) to the joy of
creating, finding, learning, and telling stories, at
campfires, slumber parties, school, libraries, family
get-togethers, and other venues.
    LCCN: 98-61152
    ISBN: 0-9638339-3-6

    1. Storytelling--Handbooks, manuals, etc.--Juvenile
literature.   I. Shupe, Bobbi. II. Title.

LB1042.D83 1999   372.67'7
                        QBI98-1412

FOR ALL THE STORYTELLERS IN MY FAMILY

AND ALL YOUNG STORYTELLERS EVERYWHERE.

ACKNOWLEDGMENTS

I would like to thank all those who contributed their help, advice, and support throughout this entire project, especially Bobbi Shupe for creating all the additional illustrations for this edition; Darryl Dubrovin for photographing the how-to pictures for the storytelling stick and the yarn doll; Corinne Bergstrom for carefully editing the manuscript; Linda White for content editing; Cathy Miller for researching some of the resource information; Ken R. Dubrovin for setting up new computers and printers and coming to my aid when the computer developed a mind of its own; and to Gilliland Printing for helping me assemble all the pieces.

And many, many thanks to my entire family for all their patience and encouragement.

Other Books By
VIVIAN DUBROVIN

NONFICTION

Create Your Own Storytelling Stories
Creative Word Processing
Guide To Alternative Education And Training
Running A School Newspaper
Storytelling Adventures: Stories Kids Can Tell
The ABC's Of The New Print Shop
Write Your Own Story

FICTION

A Better Bit And Bridle
A Chance To Win
Baseball Just For Fun
Open The Gate
Rescue On Skis
The Magic Bowling Ball
The Track Trophy
Trailering Troubles

TABLE OF CONTENTS

PREFACE

When I begin to write a book, I start gathering information. I read books, talk to people, and order magazines and newsletters. I tell everyone I meet to send me information. It's a little like turning on a radio or TV. However, when the book is published, the information does not stop coming in. It's a little like *not* being able to turn off that radio or TV.

This is exactly what happened when I wrote the first edition of *Storytelling For The Fun Of It: A Handbook for Children* in 1993 and published it in 1994. The information kept coming. Teachers shared their experiences, storytellers added advice, and kids had new ideas.

It was good information and I wished I could have included it in the book. So, in the summer of 1994, I started the *Junior Storyteller* newsletter to pass on some of this new information. Each issue contained a storytelling project.

In 1995, I wrote *Create Your Own Storytelling Story* to show boys and girls the traditional way to create tales. The book explains how to start with the two main elements—character and plot—and develop minor elements to create an exciting storytelling story.

Meanwhile, storytelling projects in the *Junior Storyteller* were becoming so successful that in 1996 I created The Kids' Storytelling Club website (http://www.storycraft.com) to send out more storytelling projects.

In 1997, I wrote *Storytelling Adventures: Stories Kids Can Tell*, which includes seven ways to have fun with storytelling projects. It was an instant success and received the best reviews of any book I've ever written.

So, when Storycraft Publishing began to run out of copies of the first edition of *Storytelling For The Fun Of It*, I suggested that I update some information, add new ideas on storytelling opportunities, and include a few popular projects from the *Junior Storyteller* and The Kids' Storytelling Club.

I hope you enjoy this new edition. There are many more pages, additional illustrations, and new how-to photos. Please continue sending your feedback. We'll pass it on in the newsletter and on the website.

Vivian Dubrovin

PART 1
A Story About Storytelling

CHAPTER 1

HOW IT ALL BEGAN

A young man strode into the village square. He stopped in front of the big statue and glanced around at the merchants selling their wares. Then he whipped off his hat and plopped it on the ground in front of him to catch a coin or two. He picked up a small banjo and strummed a few loud chords. He waited for the townsfolk to gather around him. Then he began to play and sing:

"Gather 'round ye merry folk
and listen to a tale or two..."

Long ago, before there was television, radio, newspapers, or even books, people got their news and entertainment from storytellers. Like this young man, they wandered from village to village and earned their living by telling tales. Some played instruments and sang their stories.

3

Some used magic tricks as they talked. Others depended on a simple prop or two to create a mood for their spellbinding dramas.

Then the printing press was invented and people preferred to read books, magazines, and newspapers. Later when radio came along, they wanted stories with sound effects. When movies and television became popular, people wanted to see, as well as hear, stories.

Not so long ago, in the 1970's, many people realized that they were missing something. There was a certain magic in listening to a live storyteller. So they began to tell stories again.

They had so much fun that they started to form storytelling clubs, hold festivals, and attend workshops. By 1998 the *National Storytelling Directory*, published by The National Storytelling Association, listed 293 storytelling organizations and centers, 259 storytelling events, and 159 workshops and educational opportunities.

Because adults are having so much fun with storytelling, they are now encouraging kids to get in on this artform. Families are having story times. Teachers are developing storytelling programs. Churches and youth organizations are holding workshops for children. Guilds of the National Story League are sponsoring Junior Leagues.

Boys and girls are beginning to polish up their stories, trade and collect good telling tales, and look for every chance to be junior storytellers.

CHAPTER 2 ★

KIDS TELL TALES TODAY

★ Where can kids tell stories?
★ Why are they doing it?
★ How can you get in on the fun?

Since so many kids are discovering that storytelling is a lot of fun, it is an activity that is fast becoming very popular.

Where Kids Are Telling Stories

Kids can find opportunities for storytelling in many places today. Some of those chances are part of kids' everyday activities. Some are special activities that you will have to find.

Around Campfires

Did you ever sit around a campfire, roast hot dogs, and then toast marshmallows? When the sun went down and the stars came out, did you tell stories?

Long ago in some cultures, one person was the storyteller. This person told the traditional tales that had been handed down from one generation to the next generation. Today everyone around a campfire may share a tale. Sometimes they are funny stories. Other times they are scary ghost stories.

At Slumber Parties

While many kids at slumber parties still watch videos, others are turning to storytellers. Some-times these storytellers are neighborhood adults or some-one's older brother or sister. But often the storyteller is one of the guests, a classmate or friend, who likes to tell stories and is willing to tell one of their favorite tales or create one for your special occasion.

6

In Classroom Projects

Your first experience with storytelling may be during a project in your classroom at school.

In Joshua's fifth-grade literature class, a local story-teller told some legends. She then helped the students find stories to share at a storytelling performance for their parents.

In Christine's sixth-grade class, several boys and girls learned stories for kindergarten and first-grade children. After telling their stories at their own school, they visited other schools.

Todd's fourth grade class told stories about their town as part of a study of local history. A storyteller came to their classroom, dressed as one of the town's famous pioneers, and told about homesteading, wagon trains, and why the railroad runs through the south end of town. Then each boy and girl chose one historical character or event and created a storytelling story. They had so much fun that they put on a storytelling concert for the third graders to get them interested in studying local history next year.

In Public Library Programs

You might find a storytelling workshop at your public library.

7

Like school projects, library programs often begin with a professional storyteller. Then you work with the storyteller to find and develop your own story to tell.

Public and school libraries have lots of good books with stories you can tell. Look for legends, fairy tales, folk tales, and other stories. Their storytelling events will encourage you to read the books that they have at the library.

In Heritage Programs

Heritage programs are becoming popular in schools, churches, and youth groups, such as Boy Scouts, Girl Scouts, Camp Fire, and 4-H clubs. Some Storytelling Clubs are also including them. Boys and girls explore their heritage, share legends, myths, customs, and even some family experience stories in a storytelling concert.

8

During Vacations and Car Pool Rides

On long vacation rides, some families play games or tell stories in the car to pass time. Now families that began storytelling during long trips also play story-games and tell mini-tales during car pool rides. Sometimes they make up stories that need to be continued during the next ride. It makes car pooling a lot more fun!

At Family Gatherings

After a holiday meal some families gather on a front porch to share family history.

Roberto's father always tells about his escape to this country. Dan's dad likes to tell old war stories. Carolee says she gets the best stories from her parents and grandparents during family chores or other activities. Sometimes, she admits, the stories are about "when I was your age" and *not* meant to be entertaining.

9

While Babysitting

While many babysitters happily read a bedtime story to children, other kids are discovering that special stories are the key to hassle-free

sitting. Getting kids to pick up toys, eat their meals, or go to bed, is much easier with the right story.

Debbie says she was forced into creative storytelling during a violent thunderstorm when she was trying to convince two terrified preschoolers not to be afraid of the lightning. She made up a story about cloud children with new flashlights.

Babysitters who make up their own stories when they need them are sharing their yarns with friends and collecting "sitter tales."

At Festivals

Some storytelling festivals now include special workshops for kids who want to learn how to tell stories. These workshops may be one single class or a full day of several sessions. Many classroom, library, or youth

group workshops hold a festival at the end of their storytelling project.

In Contests and Concerts

Many schools are beginning to sponsor storytelling contests and concerts. In Texas, boys and girls in second through fifth grades can compete in local, regional, and state storytelling competitions. Some Junior Story Leagues, sponsored by the National Story League, are holding storytelling concerts. Boy Scouts and Girl Scouts include storytelling activities to fulfill requirements for some of their badges.

Why Kids Tell Stories

Kids tell stories for the *fun* of it. Even shy kids are discovering a certain joy when everyone in a classroom or large auditorium is glued to their every word. On the other hand, boys and girls who love being in the spotlight are finding that this is an ideal activity for them.

It's fun to make a group of people laugh because you told a joke or funny story. And it's a different kind of fun to make their eyes grow wide or have them jump because you scared them. It's also fun to tell a story that makes people think, remember, or learn something new.

Some kids like sharing, telling and listening to stories about their hobbies and interests. Other kids enjoy the friends they make when they go to storytelling festivals and parties. Still other kids enjoy the understanding and learning they gather from the stories.

Whatever the reason that starts kids storytelling, it's the special magic that holds them, makes them want to continue, and turns them into avid storytellers.

How You Can Join the Fun

Helping you join in the storytelling fun is what this book is all about. It's full of ideas, tips, and resources to get you started. It will:

☺ Help you find stories to tell…
    with examples of stories
    with ideas for adapting old stories
    with ideas for creating new ones
☺ Give resources…
    of books of stories
    of video and audio tapes of storytellers
☺ Help you gather information…
    by playing detective to uncover local history
    by interviewing family members or neighbors
☺ Give you tips and techniques…
    for learning a story
    for practicing a story
    for telling stories
    for using costumes, props, and puppets
☺ Help you create storytelling opportunities…
    by holding a storytelling party
    by starting a storytelling club
    by having a storytelling festival

Look for storytelling opportunities wherever you can find them. And join in the fun!

PART 2

*How To Find
Stories To Tell*

Chapter 3

Three Magic Tips

★ **How do you choose a story to tell?**
★ **Why is the audience important?**
★ **How do you know if a story is right for you?**

You will read many stories before you choose one you want to tell. While you are reading, look for a short story that can be told in ten minutes or less. Seek a simple plot or main idea that has a beginning, middle, and ending. The story you choose to tell should not be too complicated.

Here are three magic tips for choosing a story to tell:

1. Find a story your audience will like.

Who will listen to your story? What do they want to hear? How many people will be in the audience? Will your audience be a few of your friends at a slumber party, 50 classmates at school, or 200 parents in an auditorium?

2. Know *why* you are telling the story.

Do you want to make someone laugh? Or cry? Do you want to frighten your audience? Or just entertain them? Maybe your story is an explanation to help your audience understand something. Or it may be educational to teach history or a new idea.

3. Find a story you like.

You must *really* enjoy the story you plan to tell because you will be working with it for a long time.

Although many storytellers think that this third tip is the most important, the first and second ones will be most helpful in selecting a story. Because your audience is so important in story selection, think about some places where you could tell stories--campouts, slumber parties, classroom programs, library projects, church and religious programs, car pool rides, family storytelling, babysitter storytime, and storytelling clubs. Read Chapters 4 through 11 to find out how to select the best story for each audience.

CHAPTER 4 ★

AT CAMPOUTS

★ **How long will you be camping out?**
★ **Who is camping with you?**
★ **What stories are best for a campout?**

Whether you camp for one night or stay a week or two, you probably will have a campfire and hopefully a campfire storytime.

It's fun to sit under the stars and listen to stories, but it's even more fun to tell them. What kind of stories do you tell at a campout?

Telling Camp Legends and History

Some camps have their own legends. If you have been to this place before, share these stories with first time visitors. Or you could read about the camp history and tell an anecdote or two.

Telling Nature Stories

If you are camping in a national, state or local park, you might want to tell a nature story. There are many legends about why plants are a certain color, shape, or why their leaves whisper in the wind. There are animal legends about how bear lost his tail, how skunk got his stripe, and the great race between rabbit and turtle.

One of Cindy's favorite nature stories is "Rabbit and The Trail Signs." She first heard it on an overnight campout. Her scout group was learning how to mark and follow a trail. Some kids planned to lay a trail for other kids to follow. At storytime the night before the trail hike, the leader told this story. When Cindy tells it at campouts now, she asks everyone to pick up twelve stones to help with the story.

Rabbit and The Trail Signs

Rabbit had been watching the campers that came to State Park for years. Every time he learned something new. His favorite thing was watching children lay and follow trail signs.

Rabbit's second most favorite thing was playing tricks on the Squirrel family that lived in the big oak tree.

Mother Squirrel always worried about her babies. The two baby squirrels would believe almost anything Rabbit told them. And Father Squirrel seldom understood anything Rabbit said.

So, one day when Rabbit had learned a few trail signs, he decided to play a game with the Squirrel family. He gathered them together under the big oak tree and explained the rules that he had learned from the children.

"Whenever you come to a spot where two paths cross, place a trail sign

18

to tell me which way to go." Rabbit put three acorns on the ground, two in a row and one on the right side. "This," said Rabbit, "means turn to the right."

(Cindy puts three stones on the ground in this pattern ∴ *and asks everyone in the audience to do the same with three of their stones.)*

"If I put two acorns in a row and one on the left side," said Rabbit, "it means you should turn left."

(Cindy puts three stones in this pattern ∵ *and asks her audience to do the same with three stones.)*

"Then," said Rabbit, "if you see only two acorns in a row, that means to go straight ahead."

(Cindy places only two stones in a vertical line : *and asks her audience to do the same with two stones.)*

19

Then, because Rabbit knew that Father Squirrel was slow and Mother Squirrel wasn't paying attention, he reviewed the instructions.

(Cindy reviews the instructions with her audience.)

Rabbit tells the Squirrel family to count to 10 to give him time to get started, then follow him. And Rabbit runs down the park trail.

When Rabbit comes to the first crosspath, he puts three acorns in the middle of the trail like this:

∴ which means what? *(Cindy lets her audience answer.)*

Then Rabbit runs down the right path until he comes to another crosspath. In the middle he places three acorns like this:

∵ which means what? *(Cindy lets her audience answer again.)*

Then Rabbit runs down the left path until he comes to another crosspath. In the middle of the trail he puts two acorns in a vertical line like this:

: and runs straight ahead. But Rabbit has saved a secret sign for last. He chuckles as he thinks of Mother Squirrel not paying attention and Father Squirrel not understanding. And then he lays out his secret sign like this:

.... *(Cindy asks her audience to use four stones for this sign.)*

Then Rabbit hides behind a bush to wait for the Squirrel family and watch what they do. Rabbit thinks that his secret sign means END OF THE TRAIL, and he plans to share his lunch of leftover acorns with the squirrels when they arrive.

When the Squirrel family starts down the park trail, Mother Squirrel leads the way. When she comes to the first sign:

∴ she remembers and says, *(Cindy lets her audience answer.)*

20

Baby Boy Squirrel leads the way to the next marker:

∴ and remembers it means, *(Cindy lets her audience answer.)*

Baby Girl Squirrel leads the way to the next marker:

: and remembers it means, *(Cindy lets her audience answer.)*

Now it is Father Squirrel's turn and he leads the way. He spots the marker before he gets there. It's a new sign. It's different and he's afraid.

"Danger!" he yells. "Rabbit is warning us of danger." He turns around. "Run back! Quick!"

The Squirrel family runs back down the path.

"Quickly! Quickly!" Mother Squirrel tells her babies. "Gather all the acorns as we leave so that nobody else runs into danger." And she scoops up the trail sign that means to go straight ahead.

(Cindy picks up two stones and asks the audience to do the same.)

They run to the next marker and Baby Girl picks up the acorns that mark a left turn.

(Cindy picks up the left-turn stones and asks audience to do the same.)

They run to the last marker, and Baby Boy picks up the acorns that mark a right turn.

(Cindy picks up the right-turn stones and asks audience to do the same.)

They run to the old oak tree and hide the acorns.

Now Rabbit, back at the bush, jumps up and tries to stop the squirrels. But since they have taken the acorns, he gets lost.

So even today, if you see a rabbit in the park, it will be running around

looking for something. If you see a squirrel, it will be gathering and hiding acorns. And, if you mark a path in the park, use stones *(Cindy holds up some of the stones)* **and never use acorns.**

Telling Trickster Tales

There are many stories where a "trickster character" tries to play jokes on people or other animals. Coyote tales from the Southwest Native American tribes are very popular. The wee folk of Ireland—the leprechauns and fairies—also like to play tricks.

Use trickster tales just as you find them or create new stories by changing the characters. Instead of a coyote, make the trickster a witch, monster or creature from outer space. You can change other characters, too. Or change the setting. Have the story take place in a big city, on a boat, or on another planet.

Changing parts of old stories is the easiest way to create new ones. Use one story as the pattern for a new one.

Creating Ghost Stories

You can change ghost stories the same way. For example, one popular ghost story pattern is the appearance of someone who has died. It usually starts with your hero character driving or walking at night and meeting a stranger. The stranger is very friendly and often needs help. The hero helps the stranger who then leaves. Later the hero finds something the stranger left or lost and tries to return it only to discover that the stranger has been dead for many years.

Elly used this pattern for her Canyon Camper story.

22

The Canyon Camper

My little brother thought the signs were silly. I know he did.

We were driving down the canyon road through the narrows. The rock walls on both sides of the road rose higher than any city building. In some places there was only room for the road and the creek that ran beside it.

Then the canyon widened. There was grass on the other side of the creek and a house and cabins.

"Is that it?" asked my mother. "Help us look for the Canyon Cabins, Elly. We should be almost there."

I looked for signs to identify the tourist lodges we were passing. But Benjie was fascinated with the green road signs that said, *In Case Of Flood, Climb To Safety.*

"How silly!" my little brother said. "What else would you do?"

We ignored him because we had spotted the Canyon Cabins.

After supper Benjie and I went to the creek to throw stones into the water.

"There's hardly any water," he said, plopping a big rock into the shallow creek.

I hopped from one large rock to another until I was out in the middle of the creek. I picked up a pretty pink stone and hopped back.

Benjie picked up a sparkling rock. We took our stones back to show Mom and Dad. They were sitting outside our cabin talking to some of the other guests. Two more people joined us, a girl a little older than me and a man older than my dad. I remember the man because he was wearing a red-and-black-checkered jacket and an orange hunting hat. It was a cool night, but not that cold. I especially remember him because he got so mad when Benjie talked again about the silly safety signs.

The man told us about a big flood. He said the river—he called this creek a river—was as high as the twisted pine tree way up on the hill. He said the

23

water came fast that night. It washed out all the buildings and even the road.

He took off his hat and ran his fingers through his stringy brown hair. He talked on and on about that terrible night of the big flood.

I was glad when Mom said it was time for bed, because the flood stories were getting pretty scary. I lay in bed and wondered about that little creek and this man's wall of water.

The next morning, as we were getting ready to leave, I saw the man's orange hunting hat still on the ground beside the chair where he had sat. Dad told me to take it to the office before we left.

My family waited in the car while I went into the office. I plopped the hat on the counter and tried to describe the man to the lady behind the desk. Her face looked very strange. She motioned to the wall behind me to a picture on the wall, a newspaper picture.

"Yeah, that's him," I said.

"That's ol' Jake Swenson. He used to own these cabins. Drowned in the big flood 20 years ago today. He tried to get all the guests to climb to safety, but he didn't climb fast enough himself. He and his young daughter died that night."

Use this pattern to create a scary ghost story for your next camp-out, especially if you are camping beside a mountain stream.

For Further Reading

Tales about how animals got the way they are can be found in collections of legends. These books are in the nonfiction section of your library. Stories about animals, such as dogs and cats, are in the fiction section. Check the library computer or card catalog. You will find a list of both fiction and nonfiction. Some books to look for are:

A Treasury of Animal Stories, by Linda Yeatman, Simon and Schuster, 1982.
Animal Folk Tales, by Barbara Ker Wilson, Grosset and Dunlop, 1983.
The Legend of the Bluebonnet, by Tomie de Paola, Putnam, 1983.

Scary stories are found in the fiction section of your library under the author's last name. Some collections of scary stories are:

Thirty Chilling Tales Short and Shivery, by Robert D. San Souci, Doubleday, 1987.
Scary Stories for Sleep-overs, by R.C. Welch, Price, Stern, Sloan, 1991.
Scary Stories to Tell in the Dark, by Alvin Schwartz, Harper & Row, 1981.
Whistle in the Graveyard: Folktales to Chill Your Bones, by Maria Leach, Viking, 1974.

CHAPTER 5 ★

AT SLUMBER PARTIES

★ **What are sharing stories?**
★ **How do you tell group stories?**
★ **How do you make a demonstration part of a story?**

Slumber parties are great places to tell sharing stories, group stories, or demonstration stories. Because slumber party guests probably know each other, they can have a lot of fun creating a story together. They may also have some of the same interests or hobbies. Since the group is small and can gather around the storyteller, everyone can see the demonstration.

Sharing Stories

Sharing stories are personal experiences. They are the things that happen to you everyday, the adventures you share with your family and friends. The stories can be about events in activities such as track, baseball, soccer, gymnastics, or other sports. They can be about things you collect, such as rocks, cards, or model toys. You can even share tales about things your parents won't let you do, times when you were afraid, or scary dreams that you have had. Tell about experiences with storytelling in school workshops or community intergenerational programs.

To get a good sharing session going, begin with a story. Then one or more of your friends will remember an experience they have had. Soon everyone will be contributing their tales.

Group Stories

In group stories, each person tells part of a story. One person creates the main character. Another tells what that character wants. A third person describes the scene.

To get the story going, write directions on small pieces of paper or cards to tell each person what to do. Number the cards so the storytellers will know whose turn it is. It's okay to be silly. The stories are meant to be funny.

On the next pages, there are some ideas for story directions. You may photocopy this page and cut on the lines. Use the paper pieces as they are or paste them onto index cards. Give one card to each guest.

As each person uses his card, he places it in the story pile. The story is over when all the cards are used up. Wild card players may use their cards at any time but must use them before card #12 has been placed in the story pile.

Story Cards for Group Story

☆ 1 The Main Character is. . .	2 The Setting is. . . ❤	3 The Time is. . . ✴	4 ◆ Other People are. . .
5 ✳ The Main Character wants. . .	6 First thing the Main ◇ Character does. . .	☆ 7 What happens to the Main Character. . .	8 What does Main Character do now?
9 What happens to the Main Character? ❤	10 How Main Character tries to fix things ☆	11 Does ✴ it solve everything?	12 How ◇ does the story end?

☆ **Wild Card** Add Another Character	**Wild Card** Add Something to the Scene ♥	**Wild Card** Add a Stinky Smell ✳	**Wild Card** Add a Bitter Taste ◇
Wild Card ✳ Add a Loud Sound	**Wild Card** Add a Nice Smell ◇	☆ **Wild Card** Add a Pleasant Taste	**Wild Card** Add a Soft Sound ♥
Wild Card Add an Animal ♥	**Wild Card** Add A Machine ☆	**Wild Card** Add Some Food ✳	**Wild Card** Add A Plant ◇

Craft Demonstrations

If you know how to make a craft, you might want to demonstrate how to do it while you tell a story. At a slumber party you could help everyone make the craft.

For example, you could demonstrate how to make a cornhusk doll, how to cut snowflake designs, or how to create shell animals or pompom critters.

Mindy told the story of The Magic Dream Doll at a slumber party while demonstrating how to make a 4-inch yarn doll. She used the instructions at the end of this chapter to create a sample.

Read the story first to enjoy it. Then read it a second time to figure out how Mindy demonstrated the craft. She did not finish the sample until the end of the story.

The Magic Dream Doll

Maria's grandmother was dying. Her hands trembled as she struggled to open the skein of yarn. Her fingers fumbled to find the loose end. Hands that once had so skillfully worked knitting needles and weaving looms now could barely pull yarn from a skein.

Maria carefully took the skein in her hands and helped to free the yarn.

"I want to show you how to make a Dream Doll," her grand-mother said softly. "I want you to know the magic."

Maria continued to pull yarn from the skein as her grandmother slowly wound it around the length of a small rectangular piece of cardboard.

"This Dream Doll is very special," her grandmother said. She paused and looked at Maria. "We have talked, told stories, shared things we like and would like to have. We have dreamed together."

Maria's grandmother stopped winding and cut the yarn. She tied one end and carefully slipped the yarn off the cardboard. About an inch from the end, she tied the yarn together again.

Maria watched carefully. The yarn looked like the tassels she and her grandmother had once made for a shawl.

Her grandmother picked up the cardboard again and began winding yarn around the width. "After I am gone," she said, "I want you to carry this Dream Doll with you to remember me."

Maria pulled out more yarn. "It will not be like you," she said.

"No," said her grandmother gently, "but it will listen to your stories. It will always listen to your dreams." She slipped the yarn off the cardboard. "There is a magic that happens when you tell your dreams to a Dream Doll." Grandmother put the doll's arms in place.

"Magic?" asked Maria.

"Magic," said Grandmother. "When you tell your dreams to a Dream Doll, they come true. They really happen."

"Oh, that's silly," said Maria. "That little yarn doll can't make my dreams come true."

"Try it," Grandmother said. "One day, you will see." Grandmother gave her the doll. "Put it in your pocket. Keep it with you."

Maria put the doll in her pocket.

After her grandmother died, Maria always wore clothes with pockets. She carried the Dream Doll in her jeans pocket. She carried it in her shirt pocket. When the weather was cold, she put it in her coat pocket.

When she felt lonely, she would slip her hand into her pocket and touch the little yarn doll. Then she would feel better. Perhaps, she thought, it was a tiny bit of magic. But she could never talk to the doll, tell it stories, or share her dreams. That, she thought, was silly.

Maria missed her grandmother very much. She missed the advice her grandmother always had for problems. She missed the stories they told each other about things that happened during the day. But most of all she missed sharing her dreams, the dreams about what she wanted to do, what she wanted to be someday.

One day, when Maria was feeling especially lonely, she reached into her coat pocket and touched the little doll. A tiny bit of magic flowed through her. She pulled the doll out of her pocket and held it in her hands. But again she could not talk to it or tell it her dreams. That, she still thought, was silly.

As her birthday approached, Maria felt worse and worse. Her birthday had always been important. Her grandmother had always planned something special.

Maria remembered last year's birthday and another one long ago. She remembered things that she and her grandmother had planned for this year. And now those things would never happen.

Days passed and her birthday came closer. Nothing happened. Nobody seemed to remember.

The day before her birthday, Maria ran all the way home from school. She pushed open the big front door and ran into the empty kitchen. She sat down in a chair, pulled the Dream Doll out of her pocket and placed it on the table.

She began to cry. Through her tears she mumbled to the doll. She told it about the best birthday she had ever had. Then she told the Dream Doll what she and her grandmother had been planning for this year and what she was really hoping would happen. She put her head on the table and cried. She cried so hard she got the little doll wet with tears.

33

The next day she had the best birthday. Everything went just the way she and Grandmother had planned, just the way she had told it to the Dream Doll.

She still carries the little doll in her pocket. Every night she takes it out and tells it about her problems. She tells it stories about what happened that day. Then she tells it her dreams.

So, keep a Dream Doll in your pocket and remember to tell it your dreams. Try it, maybe you'll see a little bit of magic, too.

After finishing the story, Mindy gave each girl at the slumber party some yarn and a 3-inch x 4-inch piece of cardboard. They all shared one pair of scissors. As the guests created their own Dream Dolls, they discussed Mindy's story.

"That *is* silly," said Sue. "A yarn doll can't make your dreams come true. Can it Mindy?"

Mindy shrugged and said, "Try it, you'll see"

Try Mindy's story and demonstration at your next slumber party.

How To Make A Dream Doll

To make a Dream Doll you will need:
- Scissors
- A 3-inch x 4-inch piece of cardboard (Any cardboard will do. You may even cut it out of an old cereal box.)
- 4-ply knitting yarn (Thin yarn works best for this small size yarn doll. Do not use a bulky yarn.)

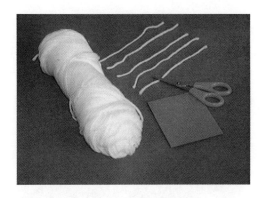

1. Cut five 6-inch pieces of yarn for tying. Put aside.

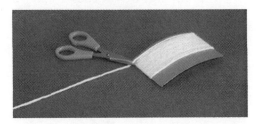

2. Wind yarn 20 times around four-inch length of cardboard. Cut end of yarn.

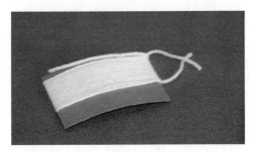

3. With a 6-inch piece of yarn, tie the strands together at one edge of cardboard. This will be top of doll's head. Gently slip yarn off cardboard.

4. With another 6-inch piece of yarn, make the head by tying all strands together about 1-inch from the first tie. This is the doll's body. Set it aside.

5. Make doll's arms by winding yarn 10 times around three-

inch width of cardboard. Cut end of yarn. Slip yarn off cardboard Tie ½-inch from each end to make hands. Use one piece of 6-inch yarn for each hand.

6. Pick up the doll body. Divide yarn strands beneath head and insert the arms between them. Using the last 6-inch piece of yarn, tie all strands just below arms to hold them in place.

7. If you want your Dream Doll wearing a skirt, cut the loops.

8. If you want your Dream Doll wearing pants, divide bottom strands in half to make legs. Cut two more 6-inch pieces of yarn to make feet by tying each leg ½-inch from the end.

For Further Reading

You can find ideas for craft demonstrations in the non-fiction section of your library on shelves marked 745. You can also find some very good ideas at your local craft and fabric stores in booklets and leaflets on how to make crafts.

Here are some examples of books you might find:

Crafts From Recyclables, edited by Coleen Van Blaricom, Boyds Mills Press, 1992.

Incredibly Awesome Crafts For Kids, Better Homes and Gardens Books, 1992.

Paper Cutting Stories A to Z, by Valerie Marsh, Alleyside Press, 1993.

Paper Stories, by Jean Stangl, Fearon Teacher Aids, 1984.

Pom-Pom Puppets, Stories, & Stages, by Marj Hart and Walt Shelly, Fearon Teacher Aids, 1989.

Storytelling Adventures: Stories Kids Can Tell, by Vivian Dubrovin, Storycraft Publishing, 1997.

The Family Storytelling Handbook, by Anne Pellowski, Macmillan, 1987.

The Story Vine, by Anne Pellowski, Collier Books, 1984.

CHAPTER 6

FOR CLASSROOM PROGRAMS

★ **Can you uncover a secret story about your town?**
★ **Is there a story in your math book?**
★ **How can mixing myth and science make a story?**

Not all storyteller stories are fiction. Some are true stories. In your classroom projects you may have a chance to explore true stories. Many school storytelling programs focus on local history, math, or science. Some school projects have holiday themes.

Local History

Few communities are lucky enough to have books written about them. In many cities, towns, counties, and states, most local history is still in the stories people tell. Finding these stories is a little like a treasure hunt. You may have to play detective to search out the facts and uncover secrets that have been hidden for a long time.

How do you know where to begin? Remember those three tips for selecting a story in Chapter 3?

1. Find a story your audience will like.
2. Know why you are telling the story.
3. Find a story you like.

Here is a time when the third one becomes most important, when YOU come first. What do YOU want to learn about?

You might want to know more about one of the town's founding fathers or the state's first governor. Why is your town located where it is? Is there a park or monument? How and why did it get there? Is there a railroad or airport? Was there a fight over where it was built?

Ideas For Local History Stories

Who started the town newspaper and why?
Why is the county or state capitol where it is?
What are the native animals? Were there ever others?
How did the first farmers or ranchers get started?
Why did the first businesses come to town?
Why is your town where it is and not somewhere else?
Where was the first school and who was its first teacher?
Was there a great flood, fire, drought in your area?
Who built the first hospital and why?
How did your town get its name?
How did the rivers or parks get their names?
Why is there a city or state park? Or university?
Who were the first people who lived in your area?

Do you or any of your friends have grandparents or great-grandparents that can remember how things were in this town when they were your age? Talk to them. Ask questions.

Old newspapers are good places to find stories about things that happened long ago. Public libraries usually have collections of old newspapers. They may be kept on film.

Be careful to not just collect a lot of facts. While they can be very interesting, facts alone are not a story.

To make a really good story, look for the reason *why* something happened. *Why* was the shopping center built on McGregor's cornfield and not in Mr. Jones's apple orchard? Is there a story about *why* the dam broke and flooded the valley? Is there a story behind the story?

Intergenerational Programs

Many schools are now including intergenerational programs into their classroom schedules. These programs vary from school to school. Some teachers, especially if they are studying local history, invite a few senior citizens to visit their class to tell personal experience stories about the town. Boys and girls may ask questions or talk with these seniors after class.

Other classes invite the seniors to contribute information and then ask the kids to create a storytelling story from the information.

In some classes students and seniors share stories about mutual interest topics such as sports, hobbies, and holidays.

A few schools invite seniors to share stories related to special study projects. When one class studied Japan, they asked a local senior citizen who had lived in Japan to tell about his experiences.

Math Stories

You can create some good stories from the math problems you are supposed to solve in math class. You know those story problems. "If John had a dollar and went to the store to buy a loaf of bread that cost 79 cents, how much change did he get?

Surely you can make this problem more interesting. Why did John need the bread? What were his choices? If he bought a cheaper loaf, could he also get a candy bar? Could he trade the candy bar?

Take this problem as an example:

> A car travels 65 miles per hour for 15 miles on
> a highway, then travels 45 miles per hour for
> 10 miles on an access road, then 35 miles per
> hour for 5 miles through town. How long will
> it take to make the trip?

Does it sound like your mom or dad asking how long it will take to drive you to a soccer game in a nearby town? Pretend it is.

Begin to turn this math problem into a story by asking questions. Who is driving? Where is that person going? Why is he making the trip?

Continue to brainstorm ideas about this drive. Is it a simple trip between two places or a detour? Why is there a detour? Do you pick up other people on the way? What is the weather today? What kind of traffic do you meet? Do you pass an accident? Does anyone in the car get sick?

When you have asked all the questions you can imagine, begin to assemble those ideas into some sort of order. Then put those ideas into story form. You could begin the story this way:

Driving To The Soccer Game

I needed a ride to the soccer game in Bentsville. It wasn't far, just 15 miles on the highway, then 10 miles into town, and 5 miles to the junior high school. Mom couldn't take me because she was driving my little sister to a drama rehearsal. Dad had to see a client, but would meet me at the game and bring me home. So Josh Hansen's dad said he would drive us both. Josh lives on the other side of our town. His dad wanted to allow a little extra time because there was a detour, a bridge out, on the access road.

Try to finish the story. When other kids find out Mr. Hansen is driving, do they all need a ride? Does he borrow a van and then rent a bus? Or does something happen at the detour? Does Josh get sick and need to be rushed to a hospital with a police escort? Think of as many things as you can to make this a very eventful ride.

You could end your story with a comment such as this:

Next week our team plays in Weston and I need a ride. Do you know anyone going that way?

Open your math book. Find a story problem. Start expanding it.

Science Stories

Exploring why things happen can produce some good stories. Why does ice melt? What if, for some reason, you had to keep a block of ice from melting. Why would it be necessary and how would you do it?

There are also some very good stories about how things were invented or discovered. Who invented the first car, train, bicycle? Why? Who discovered the North Pole? How?

Sometimes you can create interesting stories by combining ancient myths with modern scientific theory. Take an old legend about what causes thunder or lightning and combine it with what really creates this phenomenon.

Reggie combined his science project with a literature assignment to create a storytelling story of Butterfly People.

The Butterfly People

I was doing a science project when I first saw them. I was studying the butterflies in my grandmother's garden. I was also reading tales of leprechauns, brownies, and gnomes for a storytelling program in my literature class.

Mom says I got my school projects all tangled up. My grandfather says I just have a wild imagination. And he was there, mowing the grass, at the very same time.

Anyway, this is how it happened. My grandmother had given me a jar, this one right here, to catch butterflies so I could look at them closer. I had to promise to let them go when I was through.

My grandfather didn't think I needed to catch them at all. He said I should just sit very still and watch.

So, there I was, sitting in my grandmother's garden. It was a warm summer day with no wind at all. Three little orange and black butterflies were flying around, landing on one flower after another, and never staying anyplace for very long.

Maybe that's why I first noticed this special one. It landed in the pansies and stayed, as if it were resting. Then it flew across the patio to a pot of geraniums. From there, it flew to the window box of petunias.

It had the most gorgeous wings of purple, yellow, white and black. I knew that I had to capture it and take a closer look.

So I took this jar in my left hand, *like this*, and the lid in my right hand, *like this*, and I crept to that window box. The butterfly didn't see me. It was busy doing something.

I had read in a science book how hummingbirds look for nectar in flowers and how bees pollinate the blossoms. I wondered if this butterfly was looking for nectar or pollinating the petunias. Whatever it was doing, it didn't see me.

I crept closer and closer. Then, in one quick move, I scooped the jar and snapped the lid, *like this*. I had it!

It fluttered around frantically at first. Then it stood on the bottom of the jar, looked at me, and stamped its foot.

Was I surprised! I leaned close, with my eye right up to the jar, *like this*, and studied the tiny creature. It wasn't a butterfly at all. It was a tiny person with big beautiful wings and it was very angry.

I hollered for Grandfather to come see, but the lawnmower was so loud he couldn't hear me. He waved from across the yard and went on mowing.

The Butterfly Person stopped stamping its foot and sat in the middle of the bottom of the jar. I opened the jar a tiny turn and heard a teeny voice scream, "Let me out of here! How can I do my work when I'm trapped?"

"Work?" I spoke very softly.

"My story work," it screamed again.

"Story work?" I asked.

It smiled. Then it kinda glowed. "Of course," it said, slyly. "Butterfly People carry stories from one kind of flower to another."

"Were you carrying stories from the pansies to the geraniums?" I asked.

"The geraniums were very happy to hear my pansy story and gave me a good geranium one in return, which I was taking to the petunias when I was so rudely interrupted."

I thought it was a wonderful idea to carry stories from one place to another and I said so.

"Now," said the Butterfly Person, "if you let me out of this jar, I'll tell you a good story about Butterfly People."

I wanted to learn more about these fascinating little creatures, so I lifted the lid of the jar. The Butterfly Person quickly flew out of the jar and over to a rose bush.

I knew I'd been tricked. The Butterfly Person just wanted me to release it. I watched it fly from the white rose bush to the red roses to the yellow ones. I sat very still and kept watching.

It did not fly out of the garden, but flew to my shoulder. It stood close to my ear and shouted. "Butterfly People carry stories from one flower to another, from garden to garden," it said. "We travel between Mexico and Canada, north in the spring, and south in the fall. I must go now, but I will be back."

It flew around my head to my other shoulder and shouted in that ear. "You may tell your friends about the Butterfly People. Tell them to watch for us when we travel through. Perhaps one will stop on their shoulder and tell them a flower story." The Butterfly Person flew away.

I didn't believe it, of course. Mexico to Canada, indeed!

46

The next day in science class everyone reported on their observations of butterflies. Someone told about Monarch butterflies and how they migrate.

I didn't tell about my experience then. But if you ever study butterflies in your science class, look closely and you may find a Butterfly Person. It might shout a story in your ear.

Holiday Stories

How did Groundhog Day get started? What's the real history about Thanksgiving Day? What are the legends behind May Day?

If everyone in your class looks for stories about one holiday, you could have a good storytelling party to celebrate that holiday.

Don't just look at the most popular holidays. Look for the lesser known ones. Many new holidays appear every year. What about Grandparent's Day?

For Further Reading

Here are a few interesting holiday stories to get you started:

By the Light of the Halloween Moon, by Caroline Stutson, Morrow, 1993.
First Thanksgiving, by Jean Craighead George, Putnam, 1993.
Oh, What a Thanksgiving!, by Steven Kroll, Scholastic, 1988.
Hanukkah!, by Roni Schotter, Little, Brown & Company, 1990.
The Jolly Christmas Postman, by Janet & Allan Ahlberg, Little, Brown & Company, 1991.
Mr Willowby's Christmas Tree, by Robert Barry, McGraw-Hill, 1963.
The Mother's Day Mice, by Eve Bunting, Clarion Books, 1986.
A Perfect Father's Day, by Eve Bunting, Clarion Books, 1991.
Clever Tom and the Leprechaun, by Linda Shute, Lothrop, Lee & Shepard, 1988.

CHAPTER 7 ★

FOR LIBRARY PROJECTS

★ **How do you choose *one* story to tell?**
★ **Which version of a fairy or folk tale is best?**
★ **Can you combine versions of a legend to make your own?**

When you walk into a library and see shelves and shelves full of books, you know there are probably thousands of stories you could use. How do you choose one to tell?

Read, Read, Read

Read lots of books. A professional storyteller will read as few as 50 and as many as 75 stories in order to choose one to tell. That may sound like a lot of reading, but you can make this assignment fun.

If your library has a summer reading program, you can get credit for your reading while you are hunting for a story to tell.

Read Your Favorites
Start with the kind of stories that you like to read. Do you prefer mysteries, fantasy, or science fiction? Since you will have to read many stories to find the one you want to tell, pick the ones you like best.

Look for Legends or Fairy, Folk and Tall Tales
Legends, fairy tales, folk tales, and tall tales are all very good sources of stories for storytelling workshops, especially workshops held at the library.

Legends are stories that may have had some truth originally, but have been exaggerated. Tall tales are also stories that have been exaggerated, but they are fiction and have never had any truth in them.

Fairy tales are stories about magic or supernatural worlds. They usually include elves, genies, imps, sprites, gnomes, brownies, trolls, or leprechauns, as well as fairies.

Folk tales are often ethnic stories that have been handed down from generation to generation.

Picture books contain the easiest versions of these stories. Read them first.

Read about Hobbies
Perhaps you would like to read stories about your hobbies. Do you have any collections of rocks, dolls, or model cars? Are you involved in sports? Is there a new craft that you would like to learn?

50

Combining Versions to Make Your Own Tale

If you find a legend, folk or fairy tale that you might want to tell, try to find as many versions of it as you can. Read them all. Pick out the parts you like best, combine them, and create your own version of the tale. How do you do that? Let's take a look at the way Robbie created his own version for a storytelling workshop at his library.

Robbie and the Legend of The Storytelling Stone

When Robbie went to the library on the first day of summer vacation, he was looking for a nonfiction book to help him identify new rocks in his collection. Rock collecting was his favorite hobby.

He liked stories about rock collecting, too. So when he saw the bulletin board poster about a new storytelling workshop, he signed up.

The theme of the workshop was American legends. Most of his friends were talking about stories of Paul Bunyan, Davy Crockett, and Johnny Appleseed. Those were fun stories, but everyone knew them. Robbie wanted a legend that his friends might not already know.

He walked slowly down the library aisle reading the titles on the spines of the books. He took a few books off the shelves. They were collections of legends. He ran his finger down the table of contents. Imagine his surprise when he found a legend about a talking rock and another about a storytelling stone.

He sat down on the floor and began reading. He soon discovered that both stories were based on the same Seneca Indian legend. The legend told about where stories came from, about how a storytelling rock first told them to a young boy. It was a perfect story for Robbie!

Robbie carefully read both versions again and discovered that they were quite different. The first one told about a young Seneca boy who was hunting for food for his family. When he stopped to rest by a stream in the forest, the Spirit of the Rock spoke to him and bargained with him. The Rock promised to tell him stories if he would give some of his hunt in exchange. He did, and the Rock told him many stories. Then the Rock told him to take a stone or twig as a momento to help him remember each story. The next day the boy came back and traded for more stories. He came back again and again, day after day, sometimes bringing friends to hear the talking rock that told stories. Then one day the stories stopped.

As many legends do, this one went on and on and seemed to combine several stories into one legend. It began with how the Spirit got into the Rock, how the boy got a bag to carry story reminders in, and how the boy later left the town and came back as an adult.

Robbie wasn't sure where the story really began or ended. The librarian suggested that he read more versions of the legend, and she found two more books for him to read.

In another version of the story, an orphan boy was hunting food for his grandmother. When he sat on a stone to make more arrows, the stone spoke to him. He traded some of the birds he had caught for stories. The next day he brought the townspeople to hear the stone. The stone continued to tell stories for years. The stone told the boy that stories are a gift and to always request a gift in exchange for each tale. Then, when he was too old to hunt, he would be able to trade stories for food.

Robbie liked some parts of both versions. He made a list of the parts that were the same:

     1. The story was about a young boy.
     2. A large stone (rock) talks to him.

3. The stone wants some of his catch in exchange for
     stories.
4. The stone tells stories to other people, too.
5. The stone stops telling stories.

Then Robbie listed the extra parts he liked:
   1. The boy hunted food for his grandmother.
   2. The stone told him to take reminders.
   3. The stone told him to always ask for payment.

Robbie knew that a good modern story needed a beginning, a
middle, and an ending. But he also knew that the other kids in the
workshop watched TV, movies, and videos. He would have to make his
story more exciting to interest them. So Robbie began asking himself
questions to get more ideas.

   1. If the young boy was hunting food for his grand-
        mother, how did the other hunters feel? Did
        they laugh at his small bow and arrows?
   2. If he traded some of his hunt for stories, would his
        grandmother run out of food before winter ended?
   3. Could he use his stories to trade for food? How?

This is the story that Robbie told:

The Storytelling Stone

Long, long ago an orphan Indian boy was getting ready to go hunting. He pulled his small bow onto his shoulder and picked up a quiver of arrows.

"Ho! Hah!" laughed one of the hunters. "A boy is doing a man's work!" He laughed again. "Do you really think you can bring enough food home for your grandmother?"

The boy did not answer, but hurried into the forest. He was a good hunter and could get birds and rabbits, even if he couldn't bring home the big deer that the men hunters did.

He worked hard all morning and had six fat birds by noon. He sat down on a large rock to fix his arrows.

"Do you want to hear a story?" asked a voice.

The boy looked, but saw nobody. He went on fixing his arrows.

"I can tell you a story," the voice said again.

The boy stood up and looked at the stone. "Are you speaking to me?"

"If you give me one of your birds, I will tell you a story."

So the boy took one of the smaller birds and put it on the stone and he learned how the Sky Woman came to Earth.

When the story was over, the stone asked if he would like to hear another. He gave the stone another bird and learned how chipmunks got their stripes. Then he traded a third bird for a third story.

"Now," said the stone, "you must go home. But first take a black rock to remember the first story, a white stone to remember the second, and a yellow one to remember the third."

The boy picked up the stones and went home.

"Ho! Hah!" laughed all the hunters. "Three birds will not feed your grandmother this winter."

But his grandmother took the birds and said that she would dry the meat and use the feathers in a quilt.

The next day the boy went back into the forest to hunt. He got six rabbits before he came to the stone. Once again he traded rabbits for stories until he had only three left. Then the stone told him to take twigs from different trees to help him remember the new stories.

Once again the men laughed at him when he came home with only three rabbits. But his grandmother said she would dry the meat and use the fur for winter clothing.

On the third day, two of his friends offered to go with him to help him

hunt. They got six birds and six rabbits by noon when they paused at the stone to eat some berries.

But the stone wanted a gift from *each* boy in return for its gift of story. So after three stories, the boys had only two birds and one rabbit left. Grandmother took what they gave her and was happy.

Every day for the next two weeks, the three boys hunted and traded for stories. Then, one afternoon, when snowflakes began to fall, the stone told them that storytime was over. The stone reminded them to always demand a story or a gift in return for their stories and to always take a tiny memento to help remember new ones.

Winter came early that year and it was soon clear that the small amount of food the boys brought home would not last until spring.

"Let's have a storytelling feast," said the orphan boy. "Everyone can bring food to trade for stories." They had a gigantic feast and the boy told how Sky Woman Came To Earth.

Everyone liked the story and wanted to hear more. So they had another feast the next day and the boy told about how chipmunks got their stripes.

Everyday the boy traded stories for food or warm clothing, and his grandmother was never hungry or cold all that long winter.

"So this is my story," said Robbie, "and everyone who hears it owes me one in return." Robbie opened a small sack. "Here are tiny black stones to help you remember the story of the Storytelling Stone and where stories come from." He gave one to each of the boys and girls in the audience to help them begin their own story collections.

For Further Reading

Here are some legends and fairy, folk, and tall tales you might want to adapt for a storytelling workshop.

56

A Children's Treasury of Folk and Fairy Tales, by Eric Protter, Beaufort, 1982.
A Treasury of American Folklore, by B. A. Botkin, Bonanza, 1983.
Johnny Appleseed: A Tall Tale, by Steven Kellogg, Morrow, 1988.
Realms of Gold: Myth and Legends From Around the World, by Ann Pilling, CKG Publishers, 1993.
Teeny-Tiny Folktales, by Jean Warren, Warren Publishing House, 1987.
The Tales of Uncle Remus--The Adventures of Brer Rabbit, by Julius Lester, Dial, 1987.
Whopper: Tall Tales and Other Lies Collected from American Folklore, by Alvin Schwartz, Lippincott, 1975.

If you cannot find the books listed above, use the ones that are in your library. Look for legends in the nonfiction section of your library.

CHAPTER 8 ★

AT HERITAGE PROGRAMS

★ **What is a heritage program?**
★ **Are there folk tales that your relatives tell?**
★ **Can you share a religious story?**

It's easy to overlook heritage stories when you are looking for a tale to tell. You've heard these stories so many times. Yet sharing your heritage stories is a great way to discover how we are all different, how those differences each contribute to our community, and how many things we also have in common.

What Are Heritage Stories?

If you were to participate in a heritage program in your classroom, youth group, or storytelling club, you might hear the other kids say: "I'm

Irish," or "I'm German *and* Italian," or "my family comes from Mexico."

Your heritage includes your family's culture, religion, and customs.

Where to Find Heritage Stories

When you explore your background, learn about your culture, discover why your relatives came to this country, share religious stories and explain family customs, you will discover and develop some really good stories.

Exploring Your Family's Culture

You can read about your culture in books. You might start with legends, fairy and folk tales from your ancestor's countries.

Also look up ethnic costumes, dances, and songs and the stories that go with them. Why are they used and how did they get started. Are they still used today. Do your relatives remember any of the songs and dances. Could you perform them while telling a story?

Explore celebrations. Is there an independence day when that country gained independence or won a battle? Is there a harvest festival? Can your parents or grandparents tell you more about these celebrations? Do they still celebrate them?

Sharing Your Favorite Religious Stories

What are your favorite religious stories? Make a list. Ask your parents and other relatives to give you suggestions. You may uncover some that you have forgotten.

You may also want to explore stories that are the same in many religions. Look for flood stories and tales of creation.

What holidays are the same but celebrated differently? Christmas is a good example of a holiday that is celebrated many ways. How does Santa Claus or Father Christmas vary from one country to another?

Retelling The Old Stories. When spoken stories were passed from older people to younger ones, a storyteller was expected to keep the story in the original form. He couldn't change or adapt it. He simply had to remember it and retell it.

Today most of the old stories have been written down. Some have been rewritten as easy versions or picture books for very young children to read and understand.

It is these easy versions that you want to use if you are planning to do a retelling. Although you can read and use material from other versions, if you want, use the simple story as your basic outline.

You will find opportunities for retellings during your religious holidays. Religious leaders are encouraging children to tell stories as a way to learn and understand the history of their faith.

Holiday retellings are a good chance to use costumes or props to re-create a long ago setting. You might be able to add a musical instrument or background music. Some stories have puppet figures that you can buy to help tell the story.

Explaining Meanings. Sometimes you can modify a story to explain its meaning. Take the story of Noah's Ark, for example. It has been used for many different reasons. You could point out that it wasn't raining when God first asked Noah to build an ark. You could stress that

Noah did what his god asked him to do even though it wasn't what everyone else was doing. You might concentrate on the animals and Noah's concern for saving them. Or you could focus on the rainbow. There are rainbow stories in almost every culture. How are they alike? How are they different?

Sometimes you can create a new story to explain the meaning of some traditional customs. Why do you do certain things in your religious community? How would you explain them to others of a different faith? Can you make your explanation into a story?

Explaining Customs and Traditions

Your family's customs and traditions may have a religious origin, such as Passover or Easter, or a cultural basis, such as Chinese New Year. You could create a story to tell how you decorate Easter eggs or make a traditional cookie, such as a gingerbread house.

Your family's customs and traditions can be ordinary things you take for granted, such as going to your grandparent's house at Thanksgiving or a boat ride to watch fireworks on the Fourth of July.

Mandy's story of the Magic Storytelling Stick is a good example of the kind of a story you can create when you explore your family's traditions.

Mandy's Magic Storytelling Stick

Mandy loved stories. She loved to listen to her mother read bedtime stories. She loved to make up stories with her grandma. But most of all Mandy loved to listen to her great grandpa tell family tales from long ago.

How Mandy wished she could tell stories like her great grandpa. One day she even told him that.

"I wish I could be a storyteller like you, Pappy."

He chuckled. "If you want to be a storyteller, you must…" He stopped and smiled at her. "Mandy, I think you need a magic storytelling stick. I'll show you one I made long ago if I can find it. Ask your mother and grandmother if they can find theirs. It's a family tradition. It's how we all began telling stories."

At bedtime, Mandy asked her mother about her storytelling stick.

"Oh, yes," her mother remembered. "I was about your age when I made my first one. I made two more, but I don't know where any of them are now."

The next day while she was making cookies with Grandma, she asked about the storytelling stick.

"Oh, yes," Grandma said. "I was just about your age when I started to make mine. It was really magic the way it turned me into a storyteller."

That evening Mandy told her great grandpa that she had talked with her mother and grandmother about their storytelling sticks.

"I want to make one, too, Pappy. I want to be a storyteller."

Her great grandpa gave her a stick, twice as long as her ruler. Grandma gave her a piece of fuzzy yellow yarn. Together they showed Mandy how to start in the middle of the yarn at the top of the stick. Great Grandpa wound the yarn and twisted it, back and forth around the stick. Then he tied a knot.

Grandma tied two wooden beads at the ends of the yarn. "Remember, Mandy, whenever anyone asks about the yellow yarn, you must tell them our family tradition of storytelling sticks and why you are making this one."

Mandy took the stick to school the next day. When she began telling why she was making it, Archer laughed and laughed and laughed.

"How can a dumb old stick make you a storyteller?" He laughed even harder. "What's magic about a hunk of yarn wrapped around a twig?"

Mandy's teacher said it was a nice tradition and thanked her for sharing the story.

Great Grandpa was also glad she had shared the story, and he gave her some blue string from a package. Her mother gave her two tiny bells to tie onto the ends of the yarn.

The next day Mandy took the stick back to school and told how her mother and grandmother became storytellers by making their sticks. Later that afternoon, Mandy's mother gave her a red ribbon for sharing this new story.

Then Mandy told her teacher how her ancestors had made the first storytelling sticks on the boat when they came to this country to help them remember the relatives they were leaving behind. This time Archer didn't laugh. He listened.

The next day Mandy told about how, when her great grandfather was a little boy, every child in the family made a storytelling stick on the Fourth of July to celebrate coming to this country.

Archer asked Mandy if her great grandpa would show him how to make a storytelling stick.

64

When Mandy had room for only one more string on the bottom of her stick, Archer visited her home. "Sir," he said to Great Grandpa. "Mandy tells really good stories. Could you show me how to make a storytelling stick?"

Mandy's great grandpa laughed and laughed and laughed. "Archer, he said, "if you want to be a storyteller, you must tell stories."

And then Mandy saw a twinkle in her Pappy's eye. "And believe in the magic of a storytelling stick."

How to Make a Storytelling Stick

You can make a storytelling stick like Mandy did. If you demonstrate making the stick while telling the story, have several samples of the stick at different stages. Pick up each one when you come to that part.

To make a storytelling stick, you will need:
- One stick, at least a foot long. Can be a ¼ or ½-inch diameter dowel rod or a tree or bush branch.
- Six scraps of string or yarn, each about 18 inches long.
- Several small beads, tiny bells, or fancy buttons.

1. Lay first string on ground. Place top of stick in middle of string.

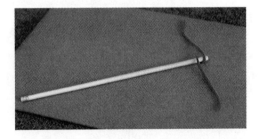

2. Bring the two ends around the front of the stick.

3. Bring two ends around back of the stick. Continue to wind string back and forth around the stick until only about three inches remain at both ends of string.

5. Tie one bead at each end of string.

4. Tie a knot in the string to fasten it.

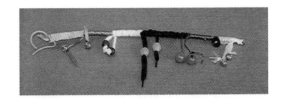

6. Repeat steps 1-5 with each string. Each piece will cover about one or two inches of the stick.

Each string represents one story. The kind of string, color, and texture should have something to do with the story. Knots, beads, or bells can also be symbolic. This helps you remember which string represents which story.

Strings You Can Use	Choosing Strings & Beads
Yarn (different colors & weights)	Where did the string/bead come from?
Ribbon (different widths)	Who did it belong to?
Twine (for wrapping packages)	Who used it?
Cord (macramé or other)	Why was it important to story?
Threads (embroidery or heavier)	Why was it important to teller?
Shoe laces (fancy colors & patterns)	Why is it important to listener?
Pony tail ties	Why will it help you remember story?

For Further Reading

There are collections of folk tales from almost every culture. Here are some to get you started.

Best Loved Folktales of the World, by Joanna Cole, Doubleday, 1983.

English Fairy Tales, by Joseph Jacobs, Dover, 1967.

Everybody Bakes Bread, by Norah Dooley, Carolrhoda Books, 1996.

Everybody Cooks Rice, by Norah Dooley, Carolrhoda Books, 1991.

Fairy Tales of Eastern Europe, by Neil Philip, Clarion Books, 1991.

Favorite Folktales from Around the World, Jane Yolen, Pantheon, 1986.

How My Parents Learned to Eat, by Ina R. Friedman, Houghton Mifflin, 1984.

Iroquois Stories, by Joseph Bruchac, The Crossing Press, 1985.

Little Folk: Stories From Around The World, by Paul Robert Walker, Harcourt Brace & Co. 1997.

My Grandmother's Journey, by John Cech, Bradbury, 1991.

My Lucky Dreidel: Hanukkah Stories, Songs, Poems, Crafts, Recipes, and Fun for Kids, by Cherie Karo Schwartz, Smithmark, 1994.

Stories of the Flood, by Uma Krishnaswami, Roberts Rinehart Publishers, 1998.

The Turnip: An Old Russian Folktale, by Pierr Morgan, Philomel, 1990.

Ukranian Easter Eggs: and How We Make Them, by Anne Kmit, Loretta L. Luciow, Johanna Luciow, and Luba Perchyshyn, Ukranian Gift Shop, 1994.

When I Was Young in the Mountains, by Cynthia Rylant, Dutton, 1982.

Why Leopard Has Spots: Dan Stories from Liberia, by Won-Ldy Paye and Margaret H. Lippert, Fulcrum Publishing, 1998.

Why the Possum's Tail Is Bare and other North American Indian Nature Tales, by James E. Connally, Stemmer House, 1985.

CHAPTER 9 ★

IN THE CAR

★ **Do you ride in the car while your relatives run errands?**
★ **Do you ride in car pools to classes or activities?**
★ **Does your family drive on vacation?**

Use the time you spend riding in a car to play storytelling games, create mini-stories, and act out finger puppet plays. It makes car rides more fun.

Storytelling Games
　　There are many storytelling games that will help you become a better storyteller. You can play voice games to help you learn how to change your voice when you pretend to be another character. You can play remembering games to help you learn stories and story patterns. You can also play singing games or make-up mini-stories.

Voice Games

One kind of voice game changes the meaning of a sentence by how you say it. You probably have asked your parents this question:

How ***long*** before we get there?
How long before ***we*** get there?
How long before we get ***there?***

Which word did you stress? Does stressing a different word change the meaning of the sentence? How many ways can you say this sentence?

Try stressing different words in the following sentences.

I just saw the teeny tiniest bug.
How long has your uncle been in France?
Did you really let her borrow your sweater?

Next time you are riding in a car, make your own sentences, and then see how many different ways you can say them.

Another kind of voice game is to pretend you are someone else. Ask or answer a question as this other person. Take the sentences above that you used to practice changing the meaning and pretend you are a football player, a policeman, a kindergartner, a mother, or a make-believe creature with a *very* different voice.

Remembering Games

You have probably played remembering games at parties. There are many of them and many kinds. One example is the Going On A Trip game. You can start the game by saying, "I am going on a trip and taking one pair of jeans." Another person in the car could say, "I am going on a trip and taking one pair of jeans and two red sweaters." A third person could add, "I am going on a trip and taking one pair of jeans, two red sweaters, and three pairs of shoes." Every person in the car should have a turn. Each person must repeat the whole list and add one more item. When one person makes a mistake, start over with a new sentence. There is no winning or losing. It's just fun, you get better, and can remember longer lists each time you play.

Another kind of a memory game is the Add An Adjective game. Start by creating a sentence, such as "I had a dog." The next person adds a descriptive word, and could say, "I had a big dog." Each person in the car must add another descriptive word. It could go on like this:

> I had a dog.
> I had a big dog.
> I had a big black dog.
> I had a big black shaggy dog.
> I had a lazy big black shaggy dog.
> I had a lazy hungry big black shaggy dog.

When you can't think of any more words, start a new sentence. Sometimes the sentences get really funny, so keep them going as long as you can. The longer you can keep a sentence going, the funnier it will be.

You can do the same thing with alliteration. This means each word you add must begin with the same letter.

Look at the mountains.
Look at the many mountains.
Look at the many majestic mountains.
Look at the many more majestic mountains.

Singing Games

There are many singing games that are like memory games. Have you ever sung Old MacDonald Had A Farm?

Singing games are good for car pool rides or field trips. Some other good ones are:

And The Green Grass Grew All Around
Found A Peanut
99 Bottles Of Pop on the Wall

If you don't know them, suggest one of these titles the next time you are on a school bus. Someone will know it and will get everyone started. Your friends will then suggest others. See how many new singing games you can collect.

Mini-Stories

Mini-stories are also games. They are created from things you see as you are riding in a car. They can start with a person, a place, or something that is happening. Create a story by asking who, what, why, when, where and how. For example, if you see a lady crossing the street, ask:

Who could that person be?

Where is that person going?
What is that person going to do when she arrives?
Why is that person going there?
When will that person arrive?
How will that person get there?

Look out the car window. The story must start with something you see. Create as many stories as you want. Everyone in the car can help.

You can also make up mini-stories by asking *what-if* or *I wonder why*. But, once again, the story must start with something you see. For example, the car may be stopped for a red light. You might ask *what if* the light never turned green. What would happen then? *What if* the road you are traveling on just ended? What would you do? See how many *what if* stories you can make up.

Finger Puppet Plays

Traveling in a car is a great time to play with finger puppets. Everyone is close enough to see your fingers move as you tell the story.

Make the finger puppets before your car ride. Make several sets for different stories. You can take these collections with you on every trip.

The best stories for finger puppet plays have five or ten finger puppet characters. You can use traditional stories or make up new stories for the puppets.

One popular traditional story is The Little Red Hen. In this tale, use your thumb for the hen and other fingers for any animals you want. For example, if you have finger puppets for a rabbit, duck, monkey, and chipmunk, use them. Remember to use a different voice for each animal.

The Little Red Hen
Finger Puppet Play

LITTLE RED HEN: I have found some wheat. Who will help me plant it?
DOG: Not I.
PIG: Not I.
COW: Not I.
CHICK: Not I.
LITTLE RED HEN: Then I'll plant it *all by myself*.
YOU: And she did.

LITTLE RED HEN: Who will help me water the wheat?
DOG: Not I.
PIG: Not I.
COW: Not I.
CHICK: Not I.
LITTLE RED HEN: Then I'll water it *all by myself*.
YOU: And she did. While the wheat grew, she asked for help again.

LITTLE RED HEN: Who will help me weed the wheat?
DOG: Not I.
PIG: Not I.
COW: Not I.
CHICK: Not I.
LITTLE RED HEN: Then I'll weed it *all by myself*.
You: And she did. The wheat ripened. And the hen asked for help again.

LITTLE RED HEN: Who will help me harvest the wheat?
DOG: Not I.
PIG: Not I.

COW: Not I.
CHICK: Not I.
LITTLE RED HEN: Then I'll harvest it *all by myself.*
`YOU: And she did.

LITTLE RED HEN: Who will help me take the wheat to the mill to be ground into flour?
DOG: Not I.
PIG: Not I.
COW: Not I.
CHICK: Not I.
LITTLE RED HEN: Then I'll take it to the mill *all by myself.*
YOU: And she did.

LITTLE RED HEN: Who will help me make cookies?
DOG: Not I.
PIG: Not I.
COW: Not I.
CHICK: Not I.
LITTLE RED HEN: Then I'll make cookies *all by myself.*
YOU: And she did. And the cookies smelled so good.

LITTLE RED HEN: Now, who will help me eat the cookies?
DOG: I will.
PIG: I will.
COW: I will.
CHICK: I will.

LITTLE RED HEN: OH NO!
            I planted the wheat *all by myself.*
            I watered it *all by myself.*

> I weeded it *all by myself.*
> I harvested it *all by myself.*
> I took it to the mill *all by myself.*
> I baked the cookies *all by myself.*
> And now I'm going to eat them *all by myself.*
> YOU: And she did, right down to the very last crumb.

Other stories you can tell with finger puppets are Chicken Little, Bremen Town Musicians, and Snow White and the Seven Dwarfs.

Little Red Hen Finger Puppets

Make finger puppets to help you tell The Little Red Hen story. Photocopy these patterns. Color the photocopies with crayons or felt-tip markers. Cut around the outside lines. Fold. Glue around top and side. Leave bottom open. When you tell the story, use your thumb for the hen and other fingers for the dog, pig, and cow. Your little finger can be the little chick.

76

CHAPTER 10 ★

AT FAMILY STORYTELLING

★ **What are family history stories?**
★ **How do you collect them?**
★ **What is a family storytelling quilt?**

A good way to uncover some interesting family stories is to start by telling a story yourself. To get a story you must give one away.

Sharing Stories

Just as you might share personal experience stories—the things that happen to you every day—with friends at a slumber party, you can tell them to your family. Take every opportunity you can find to tell a tale. These stories don't have to be long. They can be as simple as something that happened at school. Jason started a family storytelling session with one simple sentence. "I was just trying to help," he said, "and everything went wrong."

How everything can go wrong is a story pattern. You do something which someone misunderstands and they do something in response which is also misunderstood. It continues on and on.

Jason's father said it was a lot like trying to fix the plumbing in their old house. When he tried to fix one leak, something else broke. This caused something else to get bent, which caused another problem. He had to end up getting a whole new sink and cabinet.

Jason's sister told about how everything went wrong because she arrived at a meeting five minutes late. She didn't get to talk to someone before the meeting who had some new information. Everything went downhill from there.

Jason's mother told how everything went wrong because of a telephone call. His brother told about how the same thing happened to him when he forgot one piece for his science project. When Jason's friend stopped by, he jumped into the storytelling with another story.

Family storytelling time can be sharing jokes, embarrassing moments, fun things, and how, sometimes, everything works out okay.

Family History Stories

Family history stories are a little harder to collect. They may start with a single sentence, or part of a conversation. They may begin with a comment about an old photograph, trophy, or keepsake. You might have to do some detective work and interviews to get the whole picture, then create a story from the information you gather.

How to Collect Family Tales

Interviewing family members, especially grandparents, aunts, and uncles, can produce some good information. Don't walk into the room with a notepad and pencil, however, if you expect anyone to tell you ancient secrets. A casual comment usually starts the best stories.

Marsha discovered a story when she asked her mother a question while they were driving to her gymnastic lessons. She asked if her mother had ever taken gymnastics when she was a girl.

Her mother chuckled. "No. There were no gymnastic lessons in our city, but my mother, your grandmother, drove through rush hour traffic twice a week to take me to horseback riding lessons."

"Like Aunt Lisa?" Marsha asked. "She has so many trophies and ribbons."

Her mother chuckled again. "I won a horse trophy before your Aunt Lisa ever learned to ride, even before she was bitten by the first horse she ever met."

Marsha knew there was a good horse story here, but they had arrived at the gymnasium.

She didn't forget. The next day Marsha asked her grandmother about the riding lessons, and if her aunt really had really been bitten by a horse.

Grandmother didn't chuckle. She laughed loudly. "Oh my, do I remember, Marsha. The snow was a foot deep, but your mother and Lisa insisted on driving to the stables. Of course there were no lessons that day, but the girls had brought carrots for their favorite horses. Your mother's horse was polite, but Patches loved carrots so much he took a gigantic bite of Aunt Lisa's carrot and her hand. He wouldn't let go."

Grandma laughed again. "Your aunt learned how to feed carrots to horses that day. Ask her about it sometime."

Marsha made a mental note to see her aunt for more details, but she had a funny feeling that Aunt Lisa, a professional rider, might not want that story told outside the family. Instead, she asked her grand-mother about the trophy her mother had won.

When they went to look for it, Marsha and her grandmother could only find a box of Aunt Lisa's trophies, ones she had won when she was Marsha's age. Grandmother wouldn't let Marsha touch them, because they belonged to Aunt Lisa.

On Thanksgiving Day, when the family gathered at Grandmother's house, Marsha asked her aunt about the trophies. They sat down together and unpacked the box. Aunt Lisa had a special story about all but one, which Marsha's mother claimed as her long lost prize.

As Marsha suspected, Aunt Lisa did *not* want the hand biting story told. She did suggest that Marsha come to her stables, take a few lessons, and begin to create her own horse stories.

Now Marsha's mother picks her up after school and drives her across town during rush hour traffic to riding lessons at Aunt Lisa's stables. Marsha has a collection of horse tales which she shares with friends, classmates, and family. And she has a new hobby.

Conversations are seldom complete stories. You will need to create full stories from the information you collect.

Where to Look for Stories

Marsha collected some good information after a Thanksgiving dinner. Family gatherings are usually good times to talk to relatives. Have topics ready to explore at family reunions, birthday parties, anniversary celebrations, graduations, weddings, and funerals.

Topics to Explore

In our example story about Marsha and the horse story, Marsha explored the history of her aunt's hobby. Hobbies, talents and professions are good topics to consider when looking for family history stories. Other topics could include illnesses or accidents. Trips and vacations are also subjects that can turn up a good anecdote or two.

Together Time Stories

More and more families today are participating in activities and taking vacations together. They jog, ride bikes, camp, horseback ride, fish, and go boating. They take mini-trips to zoos, museums, and parks. And, they take long vacations at resorts across the country.

Informal Storytime

Since families are playing together, they are also sharing tales together. At the end of a day or the end of a trip, families share stories about what happened. Sometimes these story times are impromptu and everyone joins in to add more details or contribute "missing parts."

Formal Presentations

Some families, however, are more professional. The Smith family, for example, took a camping vacation over a four-day holiday weekend. Mrs. Smith loves to draw and brought a sketch book along with her. Mr. Smith has a hobby of recording sounds and took a tape recorder. Fifteen-year-old Brad rented a camcorder. Twelve-year-old Cora loves crafts and collected shells and rocks. Eight-year-old Mark loves bugs, beetles, worms, and furry critters. Five-year old Angela collected postcards from every place they stopped.

Everyone in this family found something special on their trip and they created a family story. They presented their story program at family reunions and holiday gatherings.

Creating Crafts and Stories

Some families are discovering that it's easier to remember and share stories while planning and creating a craft together. Other families find these same storytelling opportunities while doing chores together.

One popular craft that many families are enjoying is making and using a storytelling quilt. Some families create large traditional quilts while others make smaller lap quilts to help share their tales. There are many different ways to make a storytelling quilt.

Creating a Large Traditional Family Storytelling Quilt

Many family storytelling quilts are made with one overall picture. They may portray how a family came to this country or how ancestors traveled west in covered wagons. The family members tell stories by pointing to different parts of the quilts. These pictures are usually made with appliques (small pictures cut out of fabric and sewn or ironed onto the quilt).

Other families like to let each member create his or her own quilt block and then sew all the blocks together to make a quilt. These quilts show the diversity of family members and allow each person to tell their

84

own tales at a family gathering or individually whenever they want.

Designing a Quilt Block. Your quilt block should represent something you like to do, such as sports, a hobby, music or art.

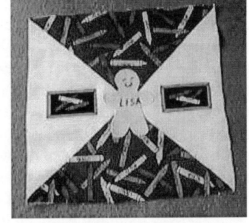

You can get ideas from novelty fabrics, materials that have pictures on them. These fabrics can be all-over designs of small pictures such as snowflakes, snowmen, holidays symbols or musical notes. Some have sports, cars, or hobby themes.

You can use squares or triangles of material with small overall

designs in traditional patchwork quilt patterns. You can tell stories about why you chose the material.

Lisa likes art projects and used a novelty fabric with crayons. She tells about different projects from each piece of fabric.

Brad is in 4-H with many animal projects, such as cows, horses, pigs and sheep. He has some very interesting stories to tell about his adventures showing some of these animals at county and state fairs. Just ask him about one of these pictures.

Jason likes sports and tells stories about baseball, soccer, and football from his quilt block.

When Eloise went to the fabric store to buy material with dogs on it to create a quilt block about her family's dog, she found material with old cars. She then remembered how her family had all gathered to clean and polish her uncle's old car for a parade, how much fun they had doing it, and how many more parades they drove the

car in. Todd found a picture of birds in front of bird houses and remembered a scout project to build bluebird houses. He quilted around the birds and houses in the picture to create a 3-D effect, and told stories about making and placing the houses to encourage bird nesting.

Making the Quilt Block. You can sew pieces of fabric together or iron on appliqués of people, animals or other objects. You can also use fabric glue.

Lisa, Brad and Jason all used a fusible backing, and no sewing, to make their quilt blocks. Each kid used the doll pattern (from the finger puppet in Chapter 11 on page 95) to put themselves on their quilt block.

Lisa cut out triangles of the crayon material and ironed them onto a white square. The small blocks are also appliques that she ironed on with fusible backing.

Brad cut out animal squares from a larger design and ironed each one onto another piece of material. Jason also cut his favorite sports from a larger design.

To learn how to use fusible backing to make any material an iron-on fabric, follow the instructions the kids used to put the doll figure onto their quilt blocks. (Always check instructions that come with the brand of fusible backing that you use.)

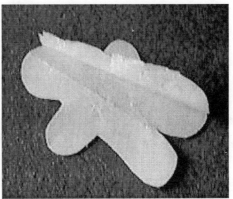

4. Peel off the paper backing. Be sure piece is cool before peeling the backing.

1. Cut a piece of fabric big enough for your pattern. Cut a piece of fusible backing the same size. Iron the backing onto the fabric.
2. Print out the pattern. Enlarge or reduce it on a photocopier.
3. Pin pattern to fabric and backing. Cut out pattern. Write your name on the fabric side.

5. Place appliqué on your quilt block and iron it in place.

You can sew all the blocks together, add the batting and backing, and quilt the whole thing just as the pioneer women did. Or you can use a more modern method that quilts each block separately, making little pillows with each quilt block. Sew them together when you have enough or when you have time. To make quilt pillows, place a layer of quilt batting between the top quilt block and the backing material. Sew around all edges with an overcast stitch.

Lap Quilts from Special Fabric

Lap quilts are similar to large traditional quilts, but are much smaller. You can put one on your lap and tell stories about it. They are easier to make and take less time.

The early pioneers made quilts from scraps of fabrics from worn-out clothes. They told stories about the clothes that the scraps came from, when they wore them, and what happened while wearing them. You can do the same thing with some of your old clothes and have fun creating both the quilt and the stories.

You could make a quilt from jeans pockets and perhaps tell stories about what was in those pockets or what fell out of them.

What about logos from old caps? Baseball or ski caps? Are there any that are out of fashion that you don't use any more? What stories do they hold? Could you cut out the design and tell how you got the cap and where you wore it?

Do you have old T-shirts or sweatshirts that you don't use anymore? Or ones that have a stain on them? Use the print panel (or part of it) from the front or back and tell why it was your favorite at one time.

How about old blue jeans? You could even use the parts with pockets and put things (like finger puppets) in the pockets and use when you tell the story.

Do you have an old scarf, one mitten or sock that has lost it's mate, or a sock that has a hole in the toe or heel but the top is still good? Use them to make a quilt and tell the stories behind these items.

Using Award Ribbons You Have Received. Did you ever receive a first, second, or third place ribbon in a sporting event? Does it still hang on your wall? Or do you have so many that they now take up a whole drawer? Several girls have used their horse-show ribbons to make quilts by sewing the ribbons in designs on a backing. One girl put her ribbons in a border around a square piece of material with horse pictures on it.

Whether your family is only your father and you; your grandmother and you; or your mom, step-dad, and six brothers and sisters, sharing stories, current or past, can be a lot of fun.

For Further Reading

For ideas on the kinds of stories you can tell about your family, you might want to read some of the following books.

A Celebration of American Family Folklore, Tales and Traditions from the Smithsonian Collection, by Steven J. Zeitlin, Amy J. Kotkin, and Holly Cutting Baker, Pantheon Books, 1982.

Abiyoyo, by Pete Seeger, Macmillan, 1986.

Homeplace, by Anne Shelby, Orchard, 1995.

Our Mountain, by Ellen Harvey Showell, Bradbury Press, 1991.

Papa Tells Chita a Story, by Elizabeth Fitzgerald Howard, Simon and Schuster, 1995.

Tell Me a Story Mama, by Angela Johnson, Orchard Books, 1989.

The Chalk Doll, by Charlotte Pomerantz, Lippincott, 1989.

The Relatives Came, by Cynthia Rylant, Bradbury, 1985.

The Stories Julian Tells, by Ann Cameron, Random House, 1981.

Story Books About Quilts

Eight Hands Round, by A.W Paul, Harper Collins, 1991.

Luka's Quilt, by G. Guback, Greenwillow Books, 1994.

Selina And The Bear Paw Quilt, by B. Smucker, Crown Publishers, Inc.,1995.

Sweet Clara And The Freedom Quilt, by D. Hopkinson, Alfred Knopf Inc., 1993.

Tar Beach, by F. Ringgold, Crown Publishers, Inc., 1991.

The Josefina Story Quilt, by E. Coerr, Harper & Row, 1986.

The Keeping Quilt, by P. Polacco Simon & Schuster, Inc., 1988.

The Patchwork Quilt, by V. Flournoy, Dial Books, 1985.

The Quilt Story, by T. Johnston & T. dePaola, Putnam & Grosset, 1985.

The Quilt, by A. Jonas, Greenwillow Books, 1984.

The Quilt-Block History of Pioneer Days, by Mary Cobb, Millbrook Press, 1995.

The Rag Coat, by Lauren Mills, Little Brown, 1991.

Adult Books About Making Quilts

Fairytale Quilts & Embroidery, by G. Harker, Merehurst, 1992.

Fast Patch Kids Quilts, by A. Hallock, & B. H. Heath, Chilton Book Company, 1996.

Story Quilts & How To Make Them, by M. C. Clark, Sterling Publishing Company, 1995.

Story Quilts: Telling Your Tale In Fabric, by M. Mashuta, C & T Publishing, 1992.

CHAPTER 11 ★

FOR BABYSITTING

★ **How can stories help you take care of younger kids?**
★ **How can custom-made tales make you a babysitter kids ask for?**
★ **What is Tabletop Telling?**

Do you babysit? Do you sometimes have trouble getting your charges to sit still? Or behave? Storytelling might be just the magic you need. And make *you* one of the most popular babysitters!

Creative Toy Stories

     Whether a child is six months or six years old, you can pick up one of their toys and create a story. It may be a simple tale about a lamb that walks around a crib. Or it may be about a teddy bear that does exercises.

The most successful stories are the ones the children help tell. Get them started by asking questions. Why is a doll or stuffed animal looking tired, or sad, or hungry today? Where is the little train going today and why? Who is coming to visit the dollhouse people?

Encourage children to tell most of the story by continuing to ask questions whenever they pause. See how long you can keep it going.

With older kids, enlist the aid of aliens from another planet. What would aliens think of the game you are playing or what would they do with a coloring book?

You might create a series of stories, a continuing saga, with one particular toy each time you sit. With a set of blocks you could build a different house for mini-monsters each time. A train set, puppet stage, or dollhouse can be the basis for stories only you create when you babysit.

Toys That Encourage Stories
Use any of these toys to tell stories with young children.

Construction blocks	**Tents**
Dollhouses	**Train sets**
Farm sets	**Cars and trucks**
Castle sets	**Crayons and paper**
Puppets	**Doctor sets**

Helper Stories

You can use a helper story, or make one up, to get kids to do what they should but don't always want to do.

If it's time for lunch and they don't want to stop playing, tell about a puppy who didn't want to eat his meal. If it's bed-time, create a tale about a hippopotamus that is looking for the best place to sleep.

If the children are afraid of a strong wind, tell a story about what causes wind and why it cannot hurt them. If they scratch themselves, try a spin-off of the tooth fairy and create a bandage fairy that rewards brave children with good luck fairy dust.

If something is lost, tell how invisible gnomes and brownies like to hide things from children and how kids can learn to find the secret hiding places.

What Is Tabletop Telling?

Tabletop telling is just what the title implies, storytelling around a table. Rather than storytelling for an audience, this is interactive storytelling. Everyone gathered around the table takes part in the telling.

You can use toys (such as model cars or airplanes), playsets (such as Lego, Lincoln Logs, or other construction blocks), or puppets. You can use a playmat on the tabletop that has city streets or airport runways or create your own setting with construction blocks to build houses, bridges, or landscapes. Your tabletop puppets will perform on this "stage" as you tell the story.

Read the story, "The Parade." Make a puppet from instructions at the end of this chapter. Try it next time you babysit young children.

The Parade
An Interactive Tabletop Story

It was a perfect day for a parade. As soon as I stepped outside, I knew it.

Walk puppet onto road. Have it look one way and then another.

I put on my parade hat and started to walk down the road.

Slowly walk puppet a few steps.

Jeannie was sitting on her front porch. "Where are you going?" she asked.

Meet another puppet (Can be boy or girl. Change name if needed.)

"I'm going to watch a parade," I said. "It's a perfect day for a parade."

Let puppet speaking move hands, turn this way and another.

"There's no parade to watch, today," she said.

Let puppet shake head or move whole body.

"There will be," I told her. "Grab a hat and come along!"

Move puppet in a come along motion.

"Sure," she said. "Parades are fun!" And she put on a parade hat.

Start puppet walking down road with new puppet following.

Walk puppet in any direction to pick up new friends. The story works best with five or more friends. If you have more than ten friends helping tell this story, you may want to tell the tale two or three times with different characters each time. Using too many characters may make a long parade, but may make your story too long.

When you have picked up all friends, walk the puppets around the playmat back to the beginning point.

When we passed my house, I took off my parade hat and sat down on the grass to watch my friends march by in the best parade I've ever seen.

Take hat off puppet and sit it down at the side of the road. Let other characters continue to march by him.

How to Make a Tabletop Finger Puppet

You can make a tabletop finger puppet that will walk across your table as you tell this story.

Slip your first two fingers into the pocket in the back of the doll to make it walk. You can draw streets on a piece of paper if you want.

1.   First photocopy the pattern.

97

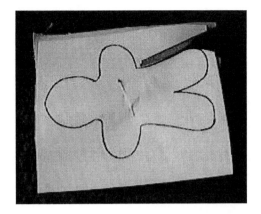

2. Pin the patterns to felt and cut out two felt puppets and one felt pocket. You may use any flesh color felt that you want.

3. Pin the two felt puppet pieces together. Position the pocket on

back and pin all three pieces together.

4. With matching color thread and an overcast stitch, sew around the puppet. Begin where the puppet's right ear would be and stitch around arm. When you come to the pocket piece sew through all three layers around the legs. Stop where the left ear would be. With felt marker, crayon or pen, draw eyes and a mouth on your puppet. If you want to draw clothes on the puppet, do that now. (You could embroider the face and clothes if you prefer.) Or, you can create the clothes from scraps of felt.

5. With a tiny amount of fiberfill, begin to stuff the puppet legs, then the arms and the head. Now finish stitching around the head.

6. The finished puppet body will look like this with the top of the pocket open for your fingers in the back.

7. You can embroider hair and clothes on the puppet. You can also glue or sew on colored felt clothes as shown here. Use yarn or curly doll hair. This sample has yarn hair.

PART 3

How To Tell
A Good Story

CHAPTER 12

MAKING A STORY YOURS

★ What if someone else tells the story you want to tell?
★ How can you make your story different?
★ How can you make each telling a special event?

No two people tell the same story the same way, and no one person tells the same story the same way twice. Each storyteller has his or her own style. A storyteller makes each telling a unique experience.

How do you make a story your very own? How can you make every one of your tellings a special occasion?

When you begin to study a story, you will have many opportunities to adapt it and make it your own. Read your story through five times, each time looking for something special.

1. Read for Fun

The first time, read for fun to capture the entire story. If there is some obvious change, make a note of it, but don't worry about changes yet.

2. Study the Characters

During the second reading, study the characters. What kind of person is the main character? Does he or she have a special voice, any unusual characteristics, needs, or wants. What about the other characters? Will you use another voice to portray them? Make notes in a notebook about the ideas you have. You may not use all or any of them, but noting your early impressions of the characters will help you learn the story and tell it better.

3. Study Story Structure

The third time, look for story structure, sequence, and plot elements. What happens? In what order? Is there a pattern of events? Do you want to add or skip anything?

4. Look for Special Words and Phrases

When you read the story again, look for special words or phrases. For example, the E-I-E-I-O in Old MacDonald Had A Farm. If there aren't any, create some to give the story more interest, to make your audience anticipate the next part or participate in a chorus.

5. Imagine The Setting

Read the story the fifth time to pick up the scene or setting. Is there anything special about the location where the story takes place? You can add details or create a scene if the original story doesn't give enough description. Don't add too many.

At this time you might want to consider if you need any story helpers? Do you want to use a costume or prop, such as a ball or bat. Do you want to sing a phrase or have any background music? Do you want to use a puppet? Will you need any signs or posters? Look at Chapter 16 for other ideas for story helpers.

CHAPTER 13

LEARNING THE STORY

★ **How do storytellers learn their stories?**
★ **What is a story map?**
★ **How can props help you remember a story?**

Some people can read a story once or twice and remember it well enough to tell it. Most people have to work a little harder.

First, remember that you *learn* a story. You don't memorize it. You may memorize an opening or closing sentence or a catch phrase or two, but never the whole story.

Make a Story Map

After you have studied and adapted the story, you are ready to make a story map to help you remember the sequence of events in the

107

story. Use either words or pictures to make this map.

A Story Map with Words

Divide your story map into a beginning, middle and ending.

Now list the things that happen in the beginning. The beginning should introduce the main character and what his problem is.

The middle of the story should include what the character does and what happens to him.

The ending should include how the character solves his problem and how the story ends.

For an example, let's use "The Magic Dream Doll" story from Chapter 5.

Beginning	Middle	Ending
Maria's Grandmother shows how to make a Dream Doll.	Maria carries doll in her pocket.	Maria cries out to the Dream Doll.
Grandmother tells how Dream Doll is magic.	She takes doll out when lonely, but cannot talk to it.	She tells it her dreams.
Maria does not believe the doll is magic.	Nobody remembers her birthday.	Her dreams come true on her birthday.
		Keep a Dream Doll in your pocket.

A Story Map with Pictures

Sometimes a story may not have an obvious beginning, middle, and ending. It may depend on an order of events. The story of "The Little Red Hen" in Chapter 9 is a good example of this kind of story.

A picture story map, like the one at the end of this chapter, helps you remember the order of events. Each picture represents something the Little Red Hen asked.

Who will help me *plant* the wheat? (shovel)
Who will help me *water* the wheat? (watering can)
Who will help me *weed* the wheat? (hoe)
Who will help me *harvest* the wheat? (basket)
Who will help me *take the wheat to the mill*? (mill)
Who will help me *make cookies*? (stove)
Who will help me *eat the cookies*? (plate of cookies)

You could create your map as a horizontal or vertical banner instead of a poster. Hang it on your bedroom wall until you learn the story. You will picture the map in your mind when you tell the story.

You can also use memory helpers or props to remember the order of events in your story. These props can be items that you place on a table and pick up as your story goes along.

Remember how Cindy used the stones as props in the story of "The Trails Signs" in Chapter 4. Laying the stones out when rabbit made the signs helped Cindy remember the order when the squirrels followed and again when they picked them up.

The Little Red Hen

CHAPTER 14

PRACTICING THE STORY

★ **How do you practice telling a story?**
★ **Can mirrors and tapes help?**
★ **Can friends and family help?**

Every storyteller practices in his or her own way. Some methods work for one person and not for another. Experiment with some of the ideas in this chapter to see what works best for you.

Every storyteller must watch for certain things during practice. One storyteller may naturally talk too fast and will need practice time to learn to speak slowly and clearly. Another storyteller may not talk loud enough. You will soon discover what things you need to watch.

Where you practice and what kind of audience you need also varies from one person to another.

In Front of Stuffed Toys or Pets

If you have a collection of stuffed animals, line them up on a table or bed as your first audience. This audience will be patient and understanding of your first attempts. And they are never too critical!

Pets sometimes listen, too. Andrea's family has a big cat named Maximillian who listens to her stories. Alex practiced his story by talking to the cows in his father's feed lot.

Greg had trouble with putting enough expression in his voice until he started telling stories to his puppy. Because the dog could not understand what he was saying, it only responded to how sad or happy, slow or fast, or loud or soft his voice was. Greg learned to change his voice often to keep the dog interested.

Before Family Members

Many kids practice by telling stories to their parents, aunts, and uncles. Grandparents often have more time to listen. Family members can help with speed and pacing. Were you talking too fast or slow for them to understand? Were you putting in extra words like "umm" or repeating words? Do you need to pause for your audience to laugh or respond?

With Friends

Encourage your friends to not only listen to your stories, but to help you become a better storyteller. Friends are great for helping you keep a story exciting. Tell them what to look for. Watch how they listen.

Are they interested? Are they excited? Are they falling asleep? Do they look around the room or work on another project while you are talking?

They may suggest hand or body movements for you to use. They may even think of props or costumes that would add interest. Get them involved in being part of your production.

In Front of Mirrors

Some storytellers practice in front of mirrors. Others do not like to watch themselves while they are talking. They say it is like trying to pat your head and rub your stomach at the same time. Try using a mirror to watch your hand gestures, body movement, and facial expressions. See if this works for you.

On Audio or Video Tape (Camcorder)

If you have a camcorder you can use or rent, make a video of your performance. Don't try to perform for the camera, however, because it doesn't respond. Tell your story to a live audience of family or friends and have someone record your performance. Play the tape back several times and look for different things each time. How can you improve it?

An audio tape recorder is very helpful. Although you cannot see yourself, you can hear what your audience hears. Can you improve the expression in your voice, speed of delivery, volume, or pauses?

At Storytelling Clubs and Workshops

Practicing in front of a group of kids who also tell stories is one of the best places to get expert help. This audience knows what to look for and can make very good suggestions. Ask for positive comments, so you can use the ideas to improve your telling.

Clubs and workshops are also good places to learn how loud you need to talk. Can you talk softly, yet be loud enough for those in the back of the room to hear?

CHAPTER 15

TELLING THE STORY

★ **How do you begin?**
★ **What if you are scared?**
★ **What if you forget something?**

Just as choosing the right story depends on when and where you plan to tell it, *how* you tell your story depends on your audience.

A story you tell to friends around a campfire will be different from the one you tell the child you are babysitting. And both will be different from the one you tell in an auditorium on parents' night.

It could be the same story, adapted three different ways. But *how* you tell it will be different, also. You need to adapt your story and your method of telling it for each audience.

115

Getting Your Audience Ready

Whether you tell your story to an audience of one or one hundred, you will have more success if your audience is ready to listen.

When Marla was getting ready to tell her finger puppet story at a slumber party, the other kids were still giggling about the jokes they had been sharing. Marla slipped her hand into her finger puppet glove, but held one finger down.

"I'm sorry," she told her friends. "I can't start yet. One of my finger puppets is still giggling."

She waited. Then, with her other hand, she lifted the finger and asked if it was ready to help tell the story.

"Hee, hee!" giggled the finger. Marla continued to wait.

When everyone else was waiting, too, Marla began.

When Luann takes her foldout castle to babysitting jobs, she always saves it for quiet time. First she lets the small children play active games to wear off some energy. Then, when it is rest time or almost bedtime, she slowly begins unfolding the castle. She asks the children to help her and they begin to talk about the characters, what kind of day it is at the castle, or what might happen there today. At this point, she has the children ready to listen to a story.

At Randy's storytelling club, one of the boys or girls lights a candle to bring storytelling magic into the room.

One storyteller likes to take small audiences on a tour through a house or building looking for the storytelling room. She leads them to a place that has been prepared for storytelling with low light and cushions.

If a real trip is not possible, you might have your audience take a pretend one with you to an imaginary storytelling place.

116

Some storytellers, when speaking to a large audience, just introduce themselves and their story because the audience is already prepared to listen. When you speak to a large group, you might give your name and the title of the story, as Jolinda did.

> "I'm Jolinda Lee Allen and I'm going to
> tell you the story of Chicken Little."

Sometimes, you may want to tell something about your story to draw the audience into it, like Pete did.

> "I'm Pete Potter and I'm going to tell
> you one of the tall tales about what
> happened to Paul Bunyan and his ox,
> Babe, one very, very cold winter day."

After an introduction like Jolinda or Pete used, you may want to pause for a few moments until your audience is listening. Count to ten or think about your character to get into the mood yourself.

If there is a catch phrase for the audience to repeat that helps you tell the story, rehearse it with them before you start. This helps get a large audience ready to listen. Let's say you are telling a story of farm animals and at the end of each part you say, "Old MacDonald Had A Farm" and your audience says "E-I-E-I-O." Practice saying the phrase and let the audience chant the response, so they know how and when to say it. Then begin your story.

Handling Problems

Every storyteller has some problem that he has to watch for or something that happens in a story that he has to overcome.

Some kids are a little nervous when they first stand up in front of a classroom or an auditorium full of parents.

Even though Kevin's teacher tried to explain that the audience was looking at his story and not at him, he was still nervous. Then he saw people in the audience who had heard the story when he was practicing. He pretended he was still practicing and tried to remember the tips they had given him. He told the story the best he ever had.

Greta, too, was terrified the first time she stood in front of her class. Then, she remembered what her aunt had said about giving your fear to one of the characters. Fortunately, this tale was a ghost story with a scary part near the beginning. But, Greta overdid it. She made her main character terrified and trembling. When she looked up and around her audience to make eye contact, everyone was glued to her every word. It was then that Greta first felt that magic storytelling feeling, the thrill of holding an audience captive. She dragged out the second scary part and skipped through the transition to the third scary part. The third part was really the hardest for her. By this time she was having so much fun it was hard to make her main character frightened anymore.

Eric had a problem in the middle of his Irish tale about the tricks of the wee folk. His audience was going to sleep. Since his tale was about the tricks elves and gnomes play on people, he continued to lull them on with sort of a droning voice. Then, suddenly, POP! Out from behind a bush jumped a leprechaun who snatched the prize and ran away. That was the end. The audience woke up to realize that they, too, had been tricked.

Michael had trouble with numbers. He knew that it didn't really matter in his story if he used five, fifteen, and fifty or one, ten and twenty. It just needed to be a growing number. But it needed to be a *reasonable* growing number.

When Michael started to tell his story at the festival, he was so nervous that he forgot the numbers he had planned to use. They just dropped out of his story as if someone had opened a trap door and they escaped, leaving all these holes in his tale.

So he improvised. When he came to the first spot, he said hundreds. When he got to the second place, he said thousands, but when he got to the third spot, he looked up, saw his older brother with hands clapped to his ears, and shaking his head.

Michael stopped, shrugged, and said his hero really had trouble counting to a million, but he was sure it was at least that many. Everyone laughed, and Michael finished his story.

Later, he learned that there were many storytellers in the audience who also had trouble with numbers or similar problems.

It is these warm, sharing moments and the thrill of holding an audience that help put the magic into storytelling and make it different than stories you watch in movies or on TV.

CHAPTER 16

USING STORY HELPERS

★ Should you use a hat or a whole costume?
★ Can you sing or draw while telling your story?
★ Would puppets help you tell the tale?

There are many story helpers that will make you less nervous or put you in the mood for storytelling. Sometimes these helpers add just the right touch to make your story something special. You won't want to use all of them, but you might want to consider one or two.

Dressing Up In Costumes

Halloween is a good time to tell stories in costume. While you are dressed as the Wicked Witch or the Good Fairy, tell a story as if your costume character were telling it. There are a lot of good Halloween stories that you could use. Look for stories that go with your costume.

Other times of the year are good for using costume, too. Dressed

as Santa Claus, you could tell how he overslept one Christmas, got lost in a storm, or found Rudolph. You might make up a short story about a pilgrim, astronaut, pirate, fireman, or soldier to use with those costumes.

Costume Parts

Sometimes you don't need a whole costume. A hat, cape, glove or jacket may be enough. Ethan used a cowboy hat and boots to tell wild west tales about Sheriff Bill and the gunman. Randy used a baseball mitt and ball to tell about the ninth inning surprise. And, Carlotta wore her bracelets, necklaces and ankle bells to weave gypsy magic.

Masks and Face Paint

A mask helps you feel like the character in your story.

While you could wear a very elaborate paper mask of a dinosaur or dragon, sometimes a simple one is just as effective. Jason made three paper plate masks to portray the parts of three characters in his story. Of course he was careful that the mask did not cover his mouth, because he wanted his audience to be able to hear his story.

Children in one workshop experimented with face paint to portray the characters in their stories. Some kids were clowns, some were animals, and a few kids were monsters. One girl even put on a traditional black-and-white mime face and tried telling her brief story using some pantomime techniques.

Using Props

Props can add to your story and keep your audience interested. Sometimes they just make you feel more at ease. They can be story reminders that help you remember which part of a story comes first, second or third.

Toni used a set of nested Matrioska dolls to tell a story about a friend's great grandmother, grandmother, mother, older sister, and baby. Netta used nested eggs to tell an Easter story.

If your story is about football, a clock, or a teddy bear, use these props as part of your story.

Adding Music or Sound Effects

If you play a musical instrument, you can use it to help tell your story. Some professional storytellers use guitars and sing their stories

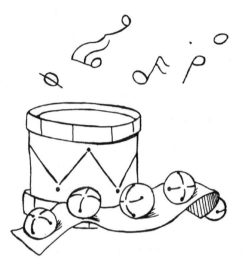

(ballads). Some only use instruments for a verse that is repeated again and again in the story.

One young girl used a flute in a story about a fairy flute player. A boy shook bells when his leprechaun appeared, because the magic creature wore bells on his shoes.

Many storytellers use drums or rattles to highlight their stories. Some boys and girls make their own drums and rattles. Look in library books for instruments that you can make.

Some storytellers use background music to create a mood. Check out sound-effect tapes. Marc used a tape of sea sounds for his surfing stories. Heidi created her own tape of eerie sounds for her ghostly tales.

Working with Puppets

Which comes first, the puppet or the story. This is a little like the chicken or the egg. With puppets, it can be either one. You may create a story for a puppet you have made or make a puppet to help tell a story.

There are so many kinds of puppets. You could use finger puppets, hand puppets, stick figures, shadow puppets or marionettes. Experiment with different kinds for different occasions.

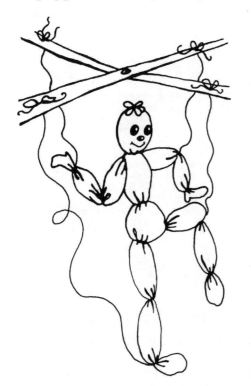

Kari used a glove of finger puppets to tell stories at parties. One family carried a box of finger puppets in their car on long vacation trips. A grandmother made several sets of crocheted finger puppets that she carried in her purse for times when she babysat. They were the right size for tiny fingers.

Drawing and Telling Your Story

On a chalkboard or large poster board you can draw as you tell your story. There are many stories designed for drawing and telling or you can create your own. Some drawings cleverly develop a unique character or scene for a special ending. Others just illustrate the tale.

Tammi's storytelling club had fun with sidewalk chalk and shadow pictures. At first they outlined each other's shadows on the sidewalk and then added details as they made up stories. Later they started posing to create monsters and silly stories.

Telling Sidewalk Chalk Stories

You don't have to be an artist to draw with sidewalk chalk while you tell a story. While telling the following story about "The Sidewalk Shadow Monster," you could make a few simple short lines for the bird and animal tracks. A couple circles can represent the cookies. The cat and dog tracks can be made with circles, too. Use your hand as a pattern (and trace around it) for the squirrel and field mouse tracks.

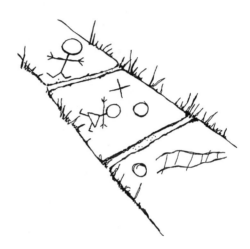

If you want to make several tracks to show the animals walking, you might want to check out some animal tracks books from your library to see how to create these patterns.

Sidewalk chalk or snow stories are fun for everyone.

The Sidewalk Shadow Monster

On a partly sunny, partly cloudy day, when the sun was dancing in and out of the clouds, John's mother asked him to help unload groceries from their van.

His mother carried one bag at a time, but John liked to carry two bags, one in each arm, like his father always did. When he reached into the van for the second bag, the one he was holding tipped. A box of cookies tumbled out, bounced on the driveway and broke open. A few cookies fell out. John didn't see or hear the cookies fall.

Little Bird was watching from a nearby tree. He saw the cookie box fall. He *loved* cookies.

As soon as John and his mother took their packages into the house, Little Bird flew down to the driveway. Soon, the sun popped out from behind a cloud and a huge shadow covered Little Bird and the cookies.

"Help!" yelled Little Bird. "The Sidewalk Shadow Monster is coming. I must warn everyone." He flew back to the tree and called to all the other birds as loud as he could. "The Sidewalk Shadow Monster is coming! The Sidewalk Shadow Monster is coming! Don't touch the cookies. The monster will get you." The sun went behind a cloud.

A cat heard the birds chattering and came to see what was happening. "Don't eat the cookies," Little Bird called down from his tree. "The Sidewalk Shadow Monster is coming! Run for your life!"

The cat ran under a bush just before a squirrel ran up to the box on the ground. Again Little Bird screamed his warning, "Don't eat the cookies. The Sidewalk Shadow Monster is coming! Run for your life!"

The squirrel ran up another tree before a tiny field mouse discovered the treasure on the driveway. Little Bird had to warn him, too. "Don't eat those cookies. The Sidewalk Shadow Monster is coming! Run for your life!"

The tiny mouse ran away before a big dog found the cookies. Little Bird called from the tree once more. "Don't eat those cookies. The Sidewalk Shadow Monster is coming! Run for your life!"

Before the dog could do anything the sun came out again and a shadow fell over the cookies and the dog. The shadow moved and a voice called out, "Good dog, Ruff! You found the lost cookies, and you didn't let anyone eat them."

John picked up the box and reached for one of the spilled cookies. "Here's a treat for a good dog." He gave the cookie to Ruff. "Come inside, now. We'll leave the other cookies for the birds, squirrels, and mice."

And the Sidewalk Shadow Monster walked into the house with the dog.

Telling the Story in the Snow

You don't have to stop telling stories outdoors when there is snow on the ground. On snowy days, tell this same story by making tracks like cat and dog tracks in the snow. Squirrel and mouse prints are easy, too. All you have to do is push your hand into the snow with fingers together to make the squirrel print and fingers apart to make the mouse paw.

Of course, whatever the weather, the best time of day to make shadow monsters is when the sun helps you make the longest shadows, usually early mornings and late afternoons. Then you can stand up at the end of the story and become the Sidewalk Shadow Monster.

Have a box of cookies to share with your audience after the story. Also, let your audience join in when Little Bird warns the animals.

Using Signs, Posters, Banners, and Flags

Some stories can use signs, posters, banners or flags. Print these out with your computer program or create them on posterboard to produce unique and fun additions to your story.

Signs help with scene or time changes. Parading back and forth with a sign can also add humor.

Cutting and Folding

Many storytellers cut paper plates or newspapers as they tell a story. The cutouts and cutups become props in their stories.

Brenda folds a newspaper in accordion pleats and cuts out dolls. She then unfolds a long chain of children holding hands for her friendship story. Sometimes she cuts out animals.

Tell a Story with Paper Snowflakes

In some classrooms, kids decorate windows with paper snowflakes during the winter months. You can tell the story of "The Snowflake That Wanted To Be a Star" to go with this window art. When you tell it, hold the main character snowflake in your hand and move it until it comes to the middle of the window.

The Snowflake That Wanted To Be A Star

Once upon a time, on a cold and frosty night, a tiny snowflake began its journey high in the winter sky. As it drifted slowly, it looked up and saw the bright stars shining.

"Oh, how beautiful they are," it whispered softly. "How I wish I could shine like that. If only I could be a star."

A big snowflake passing nearby overheard the tiny one and said, "Snowflakes are one of the most beautiful things on earth."

Another snowflake drifted closer. "Each of us is different. Look at all the lovely patterns all around you."

But the tiny snowflake looked up at the stars. "How they twinkle and glisten."

A small flake passed by on the north side. "I'm collecting circles. See my circular designs," it called out.

Another passed on the south. "I'm collecting diamonds. See me grow!"

The tiny snowflake looked around at all the snowflakes growing beautiful patterns. He knew he was growing, too. He tried to look at the stars again, but they were dim now and the sky was getting brighter.

Suddenly, the tiny snowflake landed, smack in the middle of a window.

"Oh," cried a girl on the other side. "Look at the beautiful snowflake on our window."

The sun popped over the horizon and the tiny snowflake felt its warm rays. It reflected the light and glistened with tiny star-like twinkles.

"Look," said a little boy. "This one has a little star in the middle."

The not-so-tiny-anymore snowflake felt the light flow through him. It looked at its shadow on the inside wall. The shadow had circles and diamonds and rods and slits and there in the middle, in the very center of his pattern, was a little star. The light of day streamed through it into the room with the children.

How to Make a Paper Snowflake

You can make paper snowflakes to tell with this story from white copy paper or tissue paper. You can even use coffee filters. Copy paper makes a stronger snowflake, but cutting through several layers can be difficult. Tissue paper is fragile, but allows you to create more intricate designs. Handle them very carefully.

You can make different size snowflakes by starting with different size paper. For the main character snowflake in this story, start with an 8-1/2 inch square.

1. Fold the square in half to produce an 8-1/2 by 4-1/4-inch rectangle. Fold in half again to make a 4-1/4-inch square. Fold in half to make a triangle. Fold the triangle in half again as in the picture.

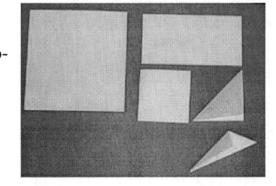

130

2. Cut off top to make a circle.

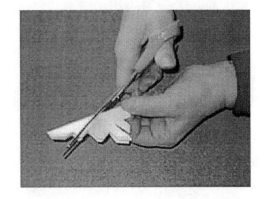

4. Cut triangles, half circles, slits, etc. to make design.

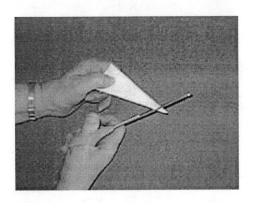

3. Snip off center to make star in middle.

5. Carefully unfold snowflake and use in your story.

For Further Reading

There are many craft books in the library. You will also get ideas by walking through a craft store or fabric shop. Look at the booklets and leaflets in these stores.

Here are a few books to give you some ideas for story helpers:

Build a Doodle, by Beverly Armstrong, The Learning Works, 1985.

Build It With Boxes, by Joan Irvine, Beech Tree, 1993.

Costumes, by Clare Beaton, Warwick Press, 1990.

Easy-To-Make Costumes, by Kathryn Harrison & Valerie Kohn, Sterling Publishing Company, 1992.

Easy-To-Make Puppets and How to Use Them, by Fran Rottman, Gospel Light, 1995.

Great Newspaper Crafts, by F. Virginia Walter, Sterling Publishing Company, 1991.

Hidden Stories in Plants, by Anne Pellowski, Macmillan Publishing Co., 1990.

I Can Draw Cars, Trucks, Trains and Other Wheels, by Tony Tallarico, Simon & Schuster, 1981.

I Want to be a Puppeteer, by Ivan Bullock and Diane James, World Book, 1996.

Make Costumes! For Creative Play, by Priscilla Hershberger, North Light Books, 1992.

Puppets, by Lyndie Wright, Franklin Watts, 1989.

The Most Excellent Book of How To Be a Puppeteer, by Roger Lade, Copper Beech Books (Millbrook Press), 1996.

Storytelling Adventures: Stories Kids Can Tell, Vivian Dubrovin, Storycraft Publishing, 1997.

Storytelling with Puppets, by Connie Champlin and Nancy Renfro, American Library Association, 1985.

CHAPTER 17

MASTERING THE ART

★ **Have you enjoyed telling a story?**
★ **Would you like to tell more stories?**
★ **Would you like to be a really good storyteller?**

Although you can read about where to tell stories, where to find stories, and how to adapt them, you must listen to live storytellers in order to master the art of storytelling.

Listen to Other Storytellers

Many adults make their living as storytellers, while some tell stories only as a hobby. Look for storytellers at local festivals, library programs, park programs, or in your school.

When you are sitting in the audience listening to a live storyteller, you have a wonderful opportunity to study both the performer and the audience. What does the storyteller do to get the attention of the audience? How does he or she weave that magic spell?

What kind of body language do the storytellers use? Watch their arms, bodies, and heads. Watch their eyes. Do the movements help tell the story or create an image?

How does the audience respond? Do they help tell the story? Are they quiet and glued to every word? Do they jump in surprise at a sudden ending?

How do you feel? Are you so interested in the story that you forget to watch the storyteller?

How does the storyteller react to the audience?

Attend a Storytelling Festival

One of the best places to find storytellers is at a storytelling festival. Every festival is different, full of surprises, and adventures.

At Large Regional Festivals in a Park

During the spring, summer, and fall months, regional storytelling guilds hold festivals in parks.

When you attend one, you'll find many tents set up. Each tent holds a surprise. One will have a registration desk where you pay to attend. Another will have a storyteller telling stories. Most festivals have a tent where you can buy books and tapes to study later. And, one tent will sell refreshments.

At large festivals, you may find two or three storytelling tents. Each will have a storyteller who tells tales for about an hour. These festivals will have a printed program to tell you who is speaking where and when. Try to listen to as many storytellers as you can. (You may leave between stories, but remember never to walk out in the middle of a story. That is considered rude.)

At Small and Local Festivals

Small festivals may have only one storytelling tent with a program of local tellers.

Many city and county fairs are adding a storytelling tent along with their other activities. Small neighborhood parks often host a storyteller. In Loveland, Colorado, the public library sponsors a storyteller who travels to neighborhood parks with a different collection of stories each week during the summer.

Look for Festivals with Special Activities for Kids

When you learn about an upcoming festival in your area, study the program or call the contact person to see if there will be special workshops for kids. Some festivals will have storytelling or puppetry workshops for kids.

Keep A Festival Scrapbook

Although you think you'll remember a festival and the tellers for a long time, you may need something to help you remember the details next year when you are preparing for your own storytelling festival.

In a scrapbook or notebook, keep records of the festivals that you attend. Include advertising flyers and newspaper articles, the festival program, photos you take or pictures that you find or purchase.

FESTIVAL SCRAPBOOK PAGE

Name of festival _____

Where it was held _____

Storytellers I heard _____

Stories I liked best
_____

Props or musical instruments used _____

Costumes used _____

How storyteller spoke_____

Body movements used _____

Did storyteller ask audience to join in? How? _____

Things I could do in my storytelling

_____

_____

_____

Photocopy the Festival Scrapbook sheet on the previous page to use in your notebook. Make notes to answer the questions.

When you need ideas for a storytelling project at school, open your notebook, flip through the mementos and read over your notes.

Treasure all the ideas you gather.

Watch Videos of Storytellers

Because it is so easy to get caught up in a story during a live performance, you may not be able to watch everything a storyteller does. Watching the "reruns" on a video tape can give you a chance to study exactly what the teller does.

If you watch a storyteller tell the story again, you will see something different, because each telling is a new event. Videos capture only one telling so you can study it closely. It is the same as football players reviewing game tapes to improve their play.

Listen to Audio Tapes

Audio tapes present stories with voice alone. Sometimes there may be a few sound effects. There is no audience and no body language to help create the image.

Listen for changes in the storyteller's voice. Does he or she use a different voice for each character? Does he or she speak loudly, then softly? How does the speed of talking make you feel?

Long car rides are wonderful times to enjoy storytelling audio tapes. Later, take the tapes into your room and play them again and again to study how the storyteller uses voice to accomplish so many things.

Story Swapping

If you want to be a storyteller, you must tell stories. Look for every opportunity to tell a story. Sign up for workshops. Join a storytelling club. Have a storytelling party.

Tell your stories. Listen and trade. Are other storytellers— adults or children—telling a story you would like to use? Talk to them. Tell them you'd like to use it, too. Storytellers swap tales all the time. A story swap might be just a casual meeting with friends. It can be any of the places listed in Chapter 2, any place you tell or listen to a story. It can be an opportunity to collect a new idea.

Creating Story Collections

As you swap stories with other storytellers, you will build your own story collection. How do you keep a story collection? How do you organize it? How do you remember which story is which?

Some storytellers have a special box in which they keep written copies, notes, and tapes of their experiences. Some storytellers keep journals or scrapbooks of their storytelling adventures.

Many storytellers are very creative in how they advertise the stories they like and want to tell. One of these creative people decorated a sweatshirt with story symbols, one for each story. Another person painted story symbols on buttons which he wore on a hat. Another storyteller had a bracelet of storytelling charms. When the collection became too long for a bracelet, she created a necklace.

Make story collecting as much fun as storytelling itself.

A Book You'll Want to Read

Although an adult book, this one is easy enough for kids to read and understand. One of America's best-known and best loved storytellers presents her favorite stories and shares her secrets for telling them in:

Jackie Tales: The Magic of Creating Stories and the Art of Telling Them, by Jackie Torrence, Avon books, 1998.

Videos to Watch

Here are some good videos that you may want to study.

Tell Me A Story, a collection of eight videos with storytellers Nancy Schimmel, Chuck Larkin, Michael "Badhair" Williams, and Beauty & the Beast Storytellers.

The Storytellers Collection, Atlas Video, Inc., 1991. Four videos with storytellers Olga Loya, Joe Bruchac, Alice McGill, and Jon Spelman.

Audio Tapes

There are many collections of stories on audio tapes for young people. Most are produced by a single storyteller.

A Storytelling Treasury, five cassettes recorded at the 20th Anniversary National Storytelling Festival, The National Storytelling Press.

Jack's First Job: and Other Appalachian Jack Tales, by Donald Davis.

News from Lake Wobegon, by Garrison Keillor.

Sing Me A Story, by Heather Forest.

Tales To Grow On, by The Folktellers.

Traditional Tales for Children, by Donald Davis.

To hear kid tellers, listen to *Stories in My Pocket: Tales Kids Can Tell,* by Martha Hamilton and Mitch Weiss, and Five Guest Kid Tellers, 1998.

PART 4
Creating Storytelling
Opportunities

CHAPTER 18

HOW TO HOLD
A STORYTELLING PARTY

★ **Is a big holiday coming soon?**
★ **Is it time for your birthday party?**
★ **Is your class planning to welcome a new kid?**

There are many reasons to have a party. Why not make it a storytelling party? You can have a storytelling party for any holiday, birthday, or special event.

The key to a successful party is in the planning. Take a little time in the beginning to carefully think about why you are having the party. Who will come? When and where will you hold it? How long will it last? What will you do? What will you eat? Once you have the answer

143

to these questions, you will be able to consider what you will need and who can help you.

Why Have A Party?

It may be Halloween, Thanksgiving, or the Fourth of July. It may be your birthday. It may be the 100th birthday of your church or youth organization. Whatever the reason for having a storytelling party, you want it to be fun.

Select a theme that goes with your reason for having the party. It can be ghost tales for Halloween, science fiction for your birthday, or historical stories for an anniversary. Tie everything to this theme. The stories you tell, the crafts you make, the invitations and favors, costumes, even the food you eat should reflect the theme.

Some themes you could consider are:

Friendship	Puppet Parade
Welcome	Crazy Characters
Ecology	Baseball
Circus	Basketball
Wildlife	Swimming
Pets	Model Mania

Use parties as a chance to experiment with storytelling. Try different things each time. What is most successful? What is most fun?

Who Will Come?

If the party is held in your class or youth group, the guest list will include everyone in that class or group. If it is a birthday or holiday party, look for family or friends that enjoy stories. Make a list of guests that get along well together.

If the party is at your home, you may want to limit the number of guests to three, five, or seven so that everyone gets to participate.

When and Where Will It Be?

Will you have the party during or after school, in the evening, or on the weekend? What time will be best for you and your guests?

Where could it be held? Could it be at your house? Is there a community center, neighborhood park, beach, or camp where you can have a party? Is a church basement, barn, or empty garage available?

Think of possible places and then check with the adults who are in charge of those locations.

The place you choose could suggest a theme. You could decorate around the theme and help create a mood for the storytelling.

How Long Will It Last?

Set a time and keep it short. Plan for an hour or an hour-and-a-half. Do not let your party run over two hours. If you think you will need more time, have another party later. Let your friends leave while they are still having fun.

Long parties tend to run into problems. Allow just enough time to do the things you plan to do.

What Will You Do?

Plan activities for every moment. What will you do when kids begin to arrive? How will you keep them entertained until everyone gets there? Is there a game you can play or songs to sing?

Janice gave everyone a balloon when they arrived at her party. She also gave them markers to draw faces on the balloons. Later they used these balloon characters in a group story.

What activities will you do first, second, and last? How will you get the storytelling started?

You can use crafts to get the storytelling started. You could have kids watch a video or listen to a storyteller.

Be sure all these activities relate to the party theme.

What Will You Eat?

Will you have a campfire or barbecue? Will you make cookies or popcorn balls that have faces and become characters for stories? Can gingerbread boys be actors before they are eaten? Decorate ice cream cones and cake squares to coordinate with your theme.

What Things Will You Need?

Carefully plan for the things you will need before the party, such as invitations and room decorations. Make a list.

Then make another list of the things you will need during the party like food and favors.

When you have your lists finished, ask a parent, leader, or teacher to check them and make suggestions for additions.

Who Can Help You?

It's best to have an adult at the party. Parents, teachers, and youth group leaders often have ideas to help your party run smoothly. Maybe you know a storyteller who could get things started or help guests learn to tell stories. It could be an adult or someone's older brother or sister.

What Kind of Stories?

Choose stories that fit your theme and purpose. Or, you could choose a theme that fits the stories you like. What kind of stories do the guests like?

If your party is to welcome a new kid in class, youth group, or neighborhood, choose stories that will help that person learn about his or her new surroundings.

If the party is to celebrate a holiday, choose stories about that special day. If you are celebrating an anniversary, look for historical stories that explain the event.

You might want to suggest that each guest bring a story to share about the theme or purpose. Ask them to let you know in advance what they are planning so that you allow enough time in your scheduling.

Party Ideas

The kind of a party you have will suggest the theme. If it is your birthday, choose a theme from one of your favorite hobbies, sports or activities.

A Monster Magic Party

When Evan decided he wanted a storytelling birthday party, he chose monsters as a theme because he loved monsters and stories about them. His friends liked weird and scary monsters, but his little sister liked friendly ones. Evan liked any kind of monster.

Evan's house had a large basement where he and his sister could do messy crafts. When Evan thought his friends would like to make monster masks or costumes, he and his mother decided the basement would be a good place for the party.

Evan had three very good friends at school, one neighborhood buddy, a cousin about his age, and two pals from swim class. He wanted to invite them all.

Since some of the kids had parents who worked and couldn't get to his house until after supper, Evan had to settle for an early evening party. He drew monster invitations with the time, date, and his address. Then he mailed them all.

Evan's mother saved old paper grocery sacks for the monster masks. Evan tried one on over his head. His mother marked where his eyes needed holes and where to cut out for his arms. Then he took off the sack and she cut the holes. He tried it on again. It was perfect.

It was Evan's job to assemble all the goodies to make the masks. He collected buttons, yarn, and fabric scraps. He found old bottles of glue and boxes of crayons. He spent a week begging recyclable odds and ends from neighbors, friends, aunts, uncles, and grandparents until he had a big box full.

Evan wanted each of his guests to make a monster mask. As they made it, he wanted them to make up things about this new monster. When they were finished, they would each wear their mask and tell a story about the monster.

Evan went to the library and collected monster stories. He read them all and selected two for his mother to read at his party.

The day before his party, Evan went to his grandmother's house to make monster cookies. He decorated each one in a different way.

Evan learned that planning the party was as much fun as the party itself.

Stories Past

When Greg's class studied local history, he found some really good stories about their town from his great-grandfather and other residents of a retirement home. When he told his teacher, his class decided to have a storytelling party at the retirement home to collect more stories.

"To get a good story, you have to give one away," his teacher told him. So Greg and two friends each found a story and practiced telling it.

The retirement home was delighted with the idea and offered to provide the refreshments.

Greg and his friends told their stories, which reminded many of the residents of some history that is not in any textbook.

The Teddy Bear Party

While Leslie was collecting stuffed toys for tots at Christmas, she decided it would be nice if her club did more than just give the toys to the kids. So she planned a storytelling party for the preschool group that was scheduled to receive the gifts. Each club member created a story to go with the toy.

At the preschool, the children were divided into small groups to hear the stories and receive the gifts. Some of the preschoolers were so excited they continued to make up stories about their animals.

Handicap Helpers

When one of his classmates was injured and needed to spend several months in a wheelchair, Doug thought a storytelling party might be a way to help his classmate. It might also educate the whole class on how to offer useful help.

Doug contacted kids who either were currently in wheelchairs or who had spent some time in one. He asked them each to tell a story about the most helpful thing anyone had done for them. They could also tell stories that included other helpful hints.

Then Doug arranged for the school auditorium for this special party because it was wheelchair accessible.

Welcome Party

When a new classmate came to Jodi's room, she decided it would be a good idea to have a welcome party. She offered the services of her storytelling club. Each member, she told the teacher, could tell the new classmate a story about some activity at school or in the neighborhood. Her teacher liked the idea and suggested that other classmates might like to join in the fun.

Mime Party

Because the kids in Ginny's workshop were not using enough hand, facial, and body movements, their storytelling coach suggested a mime party. The boys and girls painted their faces with black and white paint. They then drew stories out of a hat, and had to tell them without using any words. They could only use hand, facial, and body movements.

Family Parties

When Shelby found an old family photo album, she couldn't wait until the next family gathering. Some of the photos were just people staring at the camera, but others were quite interesting. She was sure there were some good stories. Some pictures were of babies and little children. She wondered who they were and what they were like. She wrote letters to family members and asked them to bring more pictures.

After the party, Shelby tried to write down as many things as she could remember in a storytelling journal.

For Further Reading

If you would like more ideas on holding parties with themes, you might want to look through the following books.

Great Theme Parties for Children, by Irene N. Watts, Sterling Publishing Co., 1991.

Halloween School Parties, by Wilhelminia Ripple, Oakbrook Publishing House, 1996.

How to Give Children's Parties, by Judy Williams, Smithmark Publishers, 1992.

Kids' Party Games and Activities, by Penny Warner, Meadowbrook Press, 1993.

The Disney Party Handbook, by Alison Boteler, Disney Press, 1992.

Valentine School Parties, by Wilhelminia Ripple, Oakbrook Publishing House, 1998.

CHAPTER 19

HOW TO START
A STORYTELLING CLUB

★ **Do you enjoy storytelling parties?**
★ **Did you learn to tell stories in a workshop?**
★ **Would you like to swap stories with other kids?**

You can start a storytelling club. It can be as simple as a few friends meeting on your front porch on Thursday afternoon to share jokes and stories. It can be every Friday during lunch at school and anyone is welcome. Or, it can be at seven o'clock on the first Tuesday of every month at the community center with a local storyteller.

Some storytelling clubs meet at school. After a storytelling workshop in her classroom, Marla and four of her friends started a lunchtime club. Once a week they share stories during lunch. There are eight kids in the club and they take turns telling stories.

Some clubs are spin-offs of youth groups. After a few kids in Randy's 4-H Club shared horseshowing experiences, their leader decided that these stories could help kids learn. Before the fair, his club exchanged tales about the do's and don'ts of the show ring. When kids began to stay after closing to swap additional stories, storytime became a final activity at their monthly meetings.

Boys and girls who like horses, dogs, cats, baseball, soccer, camping, mysteries, fantasy, space or science enjoy sharing tales at club meetings. Some clubs are just informal gatherings on someone's front or back porch with soft drinks and popcorn.

No matter what kind of club you want to start, take a few minutes to think about it and make some plans. Here are some questions to help you with your planning. Read them, think about them, and then make some lists to answer them.

Why Are You Starting the Club?

Why you want to have a storytelling club will determine what you will do in the club and who will join. It may help you to answer all the planning questions.

Make a list of all the reasons you can think of:

> To have fun
> To share stories
> To share tips and tricks
> To get ideas for new stories

To get ideas for props and costumes
To have a place to practice storytelling
To make friends with other storytellers
To do things as a group that you cannot do alone

Who Will Come to the Meetings?

Will you have a limited number of members? Who will they be? Include enough kids to be able to have a meeting even if some members are absent. However, the club should not be so large that everyone cannot participate at every meeting.

If there is a lot of interest and too many kids want to join, have one large monthly meeting for everyone, and also have smaller groups that meet weekly. The large group may plan some very special projects, and the smaller groups can maintain a cozy feeling.

Who else, in addition to members, could be included?

Any kids who want to come
Adult storytellers
Adult helpers
Special guests

How will you add new members?

Who Can Help You?

Where can you look for help to get your club started? Who might be able to stand by at meetings to help if there are problems?

Talk to the adults around you, especially those who work with children or youth activities. You may be surprised by how many people are not only interested in your ideas, but who are also willing to help. Consider the following people.

Parents and other family members
Teachers
Youth group leaders
Religious leaders
Community organizations
Retired people

What Will You Do at Meetings?

What you do at your meetings will depend on why you are starting the club and who will come to the meetings. Here are some possible ideas you might want to consider.

Just talk, tell jokes and stories
Have guest storytellers
Take trips to storytelling festivals
Take trips for storytelling ideas
Hold storytelling parties
Put on your own storytelling festival
Learn how to tell better stories
Watch storytelling videos
Practice new ideas
Create puppets and props
Record stories on audio and video tapes

When Will You Meet?

When you meet might depend on who is included and what time is convenient for everyone.

> During the school day
> After school
> In the evening
> On weekends

Where Will You Meet?

Where you meet might also depend on who is included.

> At one member's home
> At a storyteller's home
> At school
> In a local church
> In a community center
> In a park

How Will You Conduct Meetings?

Establish some ground rules. You may have to go back and see how you answered the first five questions before you begin.

Opening

Plan to have everyone share something when they first come. Allow time for conversation. Do you want to play a game or light a storytelling candle?

Storytime

How will you decide who will tell what story and when? You may need to have some time limits so nobody takes too long on stage.

Closing

Will you have a ritual for closing. Or will there be a snack time at the end?

Take the answers you have given to these questions and pretend you are at a typical meeting. What will happen first, second, third, last. When you think you will need something, have a problem, or cannot think of what will happen, make a note of it. Ask your parents, teachers, or friends for advice.

Do not have too many rules at first. Rules are usually created to solve problems and may not be needed in your club.

You might want to kick off your club with a storytelling party as the first meeting or as a way to get interested kids together. A club can also form after a workshop or festival to allow participants to continue the storytelling fun.

Hold An Organizational Meeting

When you have carefully thought out your plans, you are ready to have an organizational meeting. This means getting all the kids together, going over your ideas, and deciding what everyone wants to do. When everyone helps to form the club they are more enthusiastic about it.

You can begin an organizational meeting by:

1. Asking why members want to join the club. This helps you plan meetings and activities members will enjoy.

2. Asking members what they want to do. Bring out your lists of suggestions and put all the possibilities to a vote.

3. Discussing ground rules that would make everyone more comfortable. You may want to use many of the suggestions given below under "What To Expect From Members."

4. Asking members to consider three questions before next meeting. What can the group do for them? What can it do for the community? What can they do for the group?

Select a Name for Your Club

Although you could select a name for your club at the first meeting, it is best to let members think about it for a few days to come up with the best ideas. Present the idea and suggestions at the first meeting and then vote on it later. Some suggestions that others have used are:

Junior Storytellers (Plus name of town, school, church or
        organization, such as Westbrook Junior Storytellers)
Junior Folktellers
Kid Taletellers
Tale Spinners or Talespinners
Spellbinders
Storykids
Storyteens
Story Weavers or Storyweavers
Young Yarnspinners

What to Expect from Members

Everyone will enjoy club meetings and activities more if you let all kids know at the beginning that membership in this club requires some commitments from them. Some requirements for good members that other clubs have used are:

Good members come to meetings on time
Good members listen to stories
Good members volunteer to tell stories
Good members volunteer to help organize events
Good members give helpful, positive comments
Good members respect the ideas of others
Good members accept changes when needed
Good members are enthusiastic about group activities
Good members compliment others when they have done a good job of storytelling, planning, or providing refreshments

Choose Some Officers

Even though your club is just a few kids that meet once a week on your front porch, it will help if someone is in charge. That person can make sure the club continues to meet, and helps to get it started and ended on time. If your club is a larger or more organized one, you may need additional officers.

Three ways to select officers

There are three methods you can use to select the officers for your club.

160

Rotate the job. Select a system, such as alphabetically according to the first letter in the person's last name. Begin with A or Z and have each kid serve as officer for three months, six months, or a year. No longer. It's important to give everyone a chance. Kids who have held an office are more understanding of others.

Elect officers. You can decide on what officers you need. Ask for nominations and then elect them. Although this is the democratic way, it tends to put popular kids in office and often hurts less popular, but talented, members.

Appoint and approve a slate of officers. This method usually selects the most qualified people and those most willing to offer their services. Many organizations use this method. It gives a nominating committee or adult leader a chance to discuss the job with the nominee.

Officers you could have in your club

There are many officers you could have in your club. Choose the ones you need.

President, director, or manager. Call it any name, but this person is in charge. It should be someone who is responsible and can take a leadership position.

Program chairman. This person arranges activities for meetings and special events. You can appoint others to help with large projects.

Refreshment chairman. This person is responsible for seeing that there are snacks at every meeting. He or she does not have to provide them each time. A refreshment chairman may have a list of volunteers and remind them when their turn comes.

Secretary. Even if you do not want to record all the proceedings of meetings, it is a good idea to keep a record of who tells what story when. You may need to go back over such records when you plan a concert or if someone requests a storyteller from your club to tell a story for another organization or program.

Treasurer. You may only need a treasurer for special events and you can choose one at that time. Look for someone who is honest and good at math.

Establish a Club Identity

Many club members are proud of their club and like to feel that they belong. Sometimes it helps to promote this group spirit.

At one of the first meetings you can make a club banner to hang in your meeting place. It should have the club name on it and any other decorations or symbols that you want. It could list all of the members' names. Hang the banner during meetings.

You could also make club T-shirts or sweatshirts with the club name and the member's name. Get fabric paint and ideas at craft or fabric stores or ask a tee-shirt store to custom-design shirts for you.

Talk about Money

One of the joys of storytelling is that it is an activity that does not require money. You can meet and enjoy stories for no cost at all.

If your group wants to do some special things, however, you might need some cash. The club may want to collect dues, but that is not a wise idea. Money in a treasury is a temptation. When you need money you can ask for donations or earn what you need.

Some ways to get money are often more fun than the project you are trying to sponsor.

Get Donations

When you need money for a special project, start with parents. Can each of them contribute a small amount?

If you need more money than you can gather from members, look to your community. Some organizations sponsor club activities for kids and your project may qualify.

If you need specific things, try to collect used items. When one club needed costumes, they held a drive shortly after Halloween for outgrown ones. They received so many that they used what they could and then had a garage sale before Halloween the next year. Another group did the same thing to collect puppets.

Barter for Your Needs

Barter means trade. You trade something you have and do not need for something someone else has that you do need.

What could you trade? Costumes? Puppets? Stories?

Remember the story of "The Storytelling Stone" in Chapter 7? At

163

the end the orphan boy traded stories for food and clothing. How can you trade your stories?

Earn the Money

Earning money and bartering may involve the same projects. The only difference is how you are paid. When you barter you get something in trade. When you receive money as payment, you are earning it.

Look through the following list of activities, or make up your own list, to see if there is something you can do to earn money.

How to Plan Activities

When you are asked to plan activities for your club, you may think that there is no way you will be able to think of enough for every meeting. But there is a magic way to plan that will give you so many ideas you will struggle to fit them all in.

That magic way is advance planning. Take a calendar and begin planning for your entire term in office.

Special holidays

Mark the special holidays that occur in these months. Can you plan something for the meetings just before the holidays to help celebrate them? Can you plan a bigger project for the occasion?

School days off

Are there any days, such as teacher inservice days, when you and your club members do not have school? Can you plan a trip or activity to take advantage of these special days?

Community events

Mark the dates for community events such as County Fair, Fourth of July, or Winter Festival. Check with your Chamber of Commerce, City Hall, or Community Center for information on events to include. Find out if your club can participate in some of them. Allow enough time in your planning to practice and prepare stories for these events.

Storytelling festivals

Are there any storytelling festivals that are planned for your area? Will there be kid workshops included in them? Check with adult storytelling groups in your area. They will be good helpers for a lot of things you plan to do. If your local library, newspaper, and Chamber of Commerce do not know of any local storytelling groups, you may want to write to the national organization for information. Look in the appendix for names and addresses of storytelling organizations.

Museums

Check with local museums to see if they are planning any special activities or programs. Find out if your club could prepare and tell stories about the items in the museum as part of their program.

All Around Town

Check with parks, preschools, businesses, and associations. Who could use storytellers? You might even find a way to earn money for your services.

Other Schools and Storytellers

Is there a teacher who is planning a storytelling unit for her classroom who could use your help or your stories? Could adult storytellers use your help to make props? Offering the services of your club members can uncover some very interesting activities.

Additional Activities

If you need some fill-in activities for a meeting or two between special projects, you could watch videos or listen to audio tapes of storytellers. You could have everyone create a craft, such as a sock puppet that could be used in a story. You can choose a theme for the next meeting and have everyone bring a story on that theme.

Plan an event that can be held anytime. Arrange a campfire story-telling trip to a local or state park. Invite a storyteller to visit your club.

If you've scheduled all these ideas on your calendar, you may already have a pretty full program planned. Talk over these ideas with all the club members. They may know of more events that you have not yet included.

CHAPTER 20

HOW TO HOLD A YOUNG STORYTELLERS FESTIVAL

★ **Were you in a storytelling project at school?**
★ **Were you in a storytelling workshop at a community center?**
★ **Does your club want to show off its storytelling talent?**

You are now ready to put on a festival for younger kids, parents and friends. There are two kinds of festivals that you may want to consider. One is a *concert festival*. It's like a band or choral concert and is often held at the end of a school project or workshop. The other is *a festival workshop*. It's like an adult conference and is held at the beginning of a project or workshop to allow kids to explore the many opportunities available in storytelling.

How to Plan a Concert Festival

A concert festival is like a band or choral concert, but features stories instead of music. It is a concert, not a contest. You are not competing for ribbons, awards, or prizes.

In a concert all stories are enjoyed and appreciated. People come to this kind of festival to hear the tales. Your main reason for holding it should be to let the audience enjoy and appreciate every story.

Since it is a concert, you prepare for it the same way you plan a musical program. Here are some questions to help you plan your festival.

When will you hold your festival?

What is the day, date and time of your program? If the festival is at the end of a school project or workshop, it should be scheduled as a last meeting or an evening soon after the final session. If it is a stand-alone event, allow enough time for storytellers to prepare their stories and people to plan to attend. Several weeks or months might be needed. Giving yourself enough time for all the details will make the job a lot easier.

One 4-H club chose a time shortly before fair. They prepared an evening of storytelling about their experiences showing at fairs. They presented it to younger, new members who had never shown before.

Some small towns have special events like Pumpkin Pie Day, The Strawberry Festival, or a Corn Roast. You might prepare a storytelling festival to add to the activities at one of your town's gatherings.

Where will you hold the festival?

Will your festival be in the school auditorium, a meeting room at a community center, or in a park? Sometimes storytelling festivals are held at museums or historical places as part of another celebration or event.

Look for opportunities to hold mini-festivals, too. Instead of an evening or afternoon function with many storytellers, a mini-festival might have one, two, or three performers. These shorter festivals are great entertainment to feature after a luncheon, banquet, or as part of a conference. You might take stories you have already prepared, or design a program specially for an organization or business.

Why are you holding this festival?

Your festival may be a finale to a workshop or study project, but there are many other opportunities. Holiday celebrations, local tourist attractions, and heritage programs can all offer storytellers a stage.

One youth organization used members who were storytellers to tell original stories for their recruitment night program. Once a year this group invited kids who were interested in joining and their parents to come and learn more about the organization. Each storyteller told about activities that they experienced.

Who will be the storytellers?

All the participants in a workshop or class project should have a chance to tell their stories. If your event will be open to others outside your club or group, you may have to have tryouts. If you hold it together with another event, such as a banquet for businessmen, you might want to select kids who have appropriate stories for this audience.

How many stories should you include?

How many stories you need may depend on the length of the stories or the time that is available. If you are holding an afternoon festival, an hour might be all the time that is available. If you are giving an evening performance, have an auditorium reserved, and plan on an intermission, then schedule a two-hour program.

If you are telling stories to very young children, do not tell more than two or three. Keep the program short, no more than twenty minutes.

How will you arrange the program?

As you set up the program, consider who goes first, last, and in the middle. The first storyteller needs to be very good to capture the audience. This story should be a lively, happy tale, instead of a slow, sad one. The tellers who are last are usually your best. In the middle, alternate strong and weak ones, slow and fast, happy and sad. Also consider the order according to theme or length of story. Don't put two long stories together. Put a short one in between.

Prepare a printed program for your audience.

Storytellers like to see their name in print. The audience likes to know what is coming next. A printed program can be a simple list of the storytellers, titles of the stories, and the order in which they will appear.

If you have room in your program, it would be nice to write something about the storyteller and the story.

How will you get people to come?

If your storytelling concert is part of another event, someone else

170

may be responsible for advertising. If you are doing this with a club, you may need to do your own advertising. Take as much time in preparing your advertising as you take to prepare your program.

Prepare a flyer.

You can let a lot of people know about your program with a flyer. Make one 8.5 x 11-inch sign and photocopy 100 copies or more. You can make the original on your computer, or draw and hand-letter it any way you want.

Be sure your flyer includes all the important information:

> Name of the festival
> Time and date
> Location
> Price of ticket
> Phone number to call for more information

If you have room, information about storytellers and sponsors is helpful, can save many phone calls, and convince readers to attend.

Post your flyer all over town.

Now think of all the possible places you could put your flyer. Some ideas to begin with are:
> Bulletin boards at school
> Bulletin boards at community centers
> In store windows
> Library bulletin boards

You may want to give friends and family a handful of flyers to distribute to people who might be interested. Place a pile of flyers on a desk in an office or bank. Can you mail some flyers to other schools, youth groups, teams, or churches?

Who would be interested in coming to your festival? How can you reach these people with flyers?

Can you put information in a newspaper?

You might want to send one of your flyers to the local newspaper. Then call them on the phone to see if they would like to do an article about your project and maybe take a photograph. Some small town and community newspapers are especially interested in these kind of articles. Large city newspapers often are not. It is worth trying, however, because lots of people read these newspapers.

Can you place information in newsletters?

Newsletters are also a wonderful way to reach a lot of people who might want to come to your festival. If your storytelling club is part of a larger organization, find out if they have a newsletter. If you are putting on this festival with another organization, do they have a newsletter?

Check at school and the public library for other newsletters that may be interested in your project.

Allow plenty of time to get information to newsletter editors, because many publish quarterly or bimonthly.

Will there be a parade in your town?

If your festival is part of a county fair or community event, there may be a parade as part of the ceremonies. A float in the parade could be a fun way to advertise your festival.

Even if you do not have a festival planned, consider entering your club in local parades. It makes your community aware of you and may lead to requests for performances in the future.

Prepare some signs and banners for the festival.

If you are at a school, fair, museum, or other large location, how will people know where to find you?

Make large signs or banners to direct people to the right room or building. Tape the signs on the wall or put them on sticks that can be pushed into the ground. Remember to ask permission to place these.

If you cannot get permission to place signs, have one of your members, dressed in costume, at an entrance to give directions.

Create a Festival Workshop

Because storytelling is becoming so very popular, many more workshops are now available for kids. Some schools, youth groups, churches, and camps are adding festival workshops to get boys and girls interested in storytelling.

While concert festivals are performed at the end of a study unit in schools, festival workshops are presented at the beginning of a project. They are organized like adult conferences and help kids explore the many opportunities available in storytelling.

A Story Circus

The story circus is a district-wide festival workshop for middle school boys and girls to present different kinds of storytelling. Many storytellers come to teach one-hour sessions about their own styles and methods. Each session is scheduled in a different room. Although several sessions are taught at the same time, many are repeated. Boys and girls are given programs in advance so that they may choose the classes they wish to attend.

Different kinds of stories are usually offered, including myth, fairy tale, legends, mystery, science fiction, history, adventure, and personal experience. Different methods used often include dramatic telling, singing with instruments, drawing and cutting, and dancing. Some storytellers use puppets, props, and costumes.

Storytelling Crafts Festival Workshop

When some junior storytellers wanted to explore their options for using crafts in storytelling, they asked their leaders for help. What started as a small workshop by a few local artists and craftsmen grew to become a craft festival workshop. Many people in the area volunteered their time to help the boys and girls learn how to make a variety of puppets, masks, costumes, drums, bells, and other items to use with their stories.

Explore Different Kinds of Storytelling

To encourage kids to explore the many different kinds of stories and storytelling, one director opened a story circus with an adaptation of the tale of The Five Blind Men And The Elephant.

The Five Blind Men And The Elephant

Many years ago, in a far-away country, five blind men wanted to see what an elephant looked like.

One day a friend took them to meet one.

The first blind man walked up to the elephant, reached out, and touched its trunk. "Oh," he said. "An elephant is like a fat snake."

The second blind man walked up to the elephant, reached out, and touched its tusk. "Oh, no," he said. "An elephant has a hard shell like a turtle."

While the first two were arguing, the third blind man walked up to the elephant, reached out, and touched its ear. "Oh, no," he said. "An elephant is flat like a bird's wing."

While the first three were arguing, the fourth blind man walked to the rear of the elephant. When he reached out, he touched its tail. "Oh, no," he said. "An elephant is like a skinny stick."

While the other four were arguing, the fifth blind man walked up to the elephant. He reached out and touched its side. "Oh, my," he said. "It's much bigger, it's so much more."

Then the fifth blind man touched the elephant's ear, ran his hand down the animal's trunk, and felt its tusk. Without waiting to touch the tail, he said, "Yes, my friends, it is as you say. It is like a fat snake, a turtle shell, a bird's wing, and a skinny stick. It is all of this. But it is also *very much more!*"

Storytelling is a lot like this elephant. There are many different kinds of stories and many different ways of telling them. Storytelling is all of this. And it is also *very much more!*

Explore all storytelling. There is a special place waiting for you.

CONTESTS, PROGRAMS, AND OTHER RESOURCES

★ **How do you find contests to enter?**
★ **Can you join a storytelling club?**
★ **Is there a scout badge for storytelling?**

Many schools, some youth organizations, and national storytelling leagues are beginning to sponsor storytelling contests and concerts for boys and girls. You may find that opportunities already exist in your community. How do you find them? Here are a few places to look.

National Storytelling Youth Olympics
    This annual competition is sponsored by the Master's Degree Program Option in Reading/Storytelling at East Tennessee State Univer-

sity. Kids participate in local contests and then send videotapes of their presentation to the state and then regional judges. A national committee invites finalists to come to the ESTU campus for the National Storytelling Youth Olympics.

University Interscholastic League

If you live in Texas and are in grades 2-5, you may be able to enter one of the competitions sponsored by the UIL. There are local contests in schools and district competitions. Finalists travel to Austin for the state judging. Ask your teacher or school librarian how your school can get involved.

Junior Story Leagues (NSL)

The National Story League sponsors many Junior Story Leagues across the country. These groups meet like clubs to learn how to tell stories. They often do volunteer storytelling at nursing homes and present concerts at community events. For information on your nearest Junior Story League, contact Pat Langdell, 1756 14th Avenue, San Francisco, CA 94122.

Badge Projects in Scout Programs

At the time of this printing there is no badge for storytelling in either the Boy Scout or Girl Scout programs. However, there is a storytelling opportunity in almost every badge requirement.

Storytelling for Girl Scouts Look carefully through your badge book and note every opportunity for storytelling. Here's a few to get you started. In Folk Arts you can "Learn something about the tradition of storytelling...Read a fairy tale, myth, or legend that you like and be able to tell it to a group, perhaps as part of a ceremony or special event." Under Popular Arts you can "Learn tales and legends from three countries. Using these tales and legends, create a puppet show...or conduct a storytelling hour for younger children." Under Theater, you can do many activities to learn dramatic techniques. You can also create puppets, a shadowgraph, or marionettes, write your own play, and act it out for another group. Check out Doing Hobbies and Across Generations for more storytelling opportunities. What more can you find? Be creative.

Storytelling for Boy Scouts Look carefully through your badge requirements and make a note of every opportunity to include or substitute storytelling. When your requirement asks for you to "explain how" or "show why," you can use a story as an example. When it says "tell about," you can also tell a story. History can be a story. Safety rules can be presented more dramatically in story. Under Computers, you can access storytelling websites for part of the badge requirements. Can storytelling help to fulfill the Theater badge requirements? How creative can you be?

Intergenerational Storytelling at Senior Centers

Your local Senior Center may not be a place you would consider for a kids' storytelling program, but that's exactly what some of them are conducting. Intergenerational Storytelling means adults and kids sharing stories. Listening to an adult story can remind you of one and yours can trigger a good one from a senior citizen. There are many different kinds of intergenerational programs. Look for ones where both of you tell tales.

You can also find these programs at public libraries and community centers. A telephone call to your local library, community or senior center may locate a fun program for you.

Storytelling Organizations

The National Storytelling Association is an adult organization for professional storytellers. They publish an international directory which includes a listing of adult storytellers, educational opportunities, story-telling events, organizations and centers, and periodicals and production companies. They sponsor a national storytelling festival each year in Jonesborough, Tennessee. You can write for more information at NSA, P.O. 309, Jonesborough, TN 37659.

Storytelling Publications

There are many storytelling newsletters and magazines. Many of them are local and regional. Here are a few national ones:

Junior Storyteller is a quarterly newsletter for boys and girls, age 9-12. It is published by the same company and author that produced this book. It features a new storytelling project in each issue, news of kids' storytelling activities. You can send for a free sample copy by writing to Storycraft Publishing, P.O. Box 205, Masonville, CO. (You can also photocopy the coupon page at the back of this book.)

Storytelling Magazine is a publication for adult professional storytellers published by The National Storytelling Association, P.O. 309,

Jonesborough, TN 37659. There may be copies in your local library or neighborhood book store.

Storytelling World, another publication for adult storytellers, is published by the Master's Degree Program Option in Reading/ Storytelling at East Tennessee State University, ETSU Box 70647, Johnson City, TN 37659.

Storytelling Websites

One of the best ways to find current information about storytelling events and programs is through the Internet. Here are a couple sites that will get you started in the right direction.

The Kids' Storytelling Club (http://www.storycraft.com) website is sponsored by the publisher of this book and edited by the author, Vivian Dubrovin. It contains seven pages, including a "Where Can I Find?" page of information. A new storytelling project is posted each month. On the Join Page, you can get a free copy of the *Junior Storyteller* newsletter. Check it out. For more information, see last page of this book.

Storynet (http://www.storynet.org) is the website of the National Storytelling Association and is the online version of their directory. It maintains a current listing of events and activities.

New Programs

There are new storytelling programs starting every day. The best advice is to keep asking. Who sponsors after school or summer classes for kids in your area? YMCA? Community Center? School District? Call and ask if they have a storytelling workshop for kids? Don't just read the list of things they offer. Ask! When they know there is interest, they will create the workshop, class, or program that you need.

INDEX

Come Visit

The Kids' Storytelling Club
on the World Wide Web
http://www.storycraft.com

When you turn on your computer, access the Internet, and type in our World Wide Web address, you will visit The Kids' Storytelling Club. The first page you see is this picture of a young dragon telling stories to little hatchlings. You can click on several "hot spots" to travel to other pages for storytelling hints, tips, and ideas. Jump to the Welcome page and learn about these other pages or go directly to one of them. On the Create page you will get tips for creating your own stories. On Activities, you will learn how to tell your own stories. On Crafts, you'll learn how to make props to use with your stories. Check out the Where Can I Find... for information on past issues and upcoming events. Then Join the Club, get a free sample of the *Junior Storyteller* newsletter, and discover additional resources.

Come visit our web site and check us out.

Would you like to...

✗ Learn how to make glove puppets, a topsy turvy doll, and a story pillow?

✗ Discover how a tiny cube can create marvelous magic in a story?

✗ Create stories with cookies?

✗ Project excitement with shadow puppets?

✗ Learn how to write and use a storytelling script?

Storytelling Adventures: Stories Kids Can Tell shows young storytellers how to create their own props and use them to enhance their performances.

Create Your Own Storytelling Stories helps you turn events in your life into performance telling tales. Find ideas on props, customizing tales, and publicity.

Junior Storyteller is a quarterly newsletter filled with new ideas for storytelling activities.

Please send me:

$14.95

____ Storytelling Adventures $14.95

____ Create Your Own Storytelling Stories $12.95

____ Subscriptions to Junior Storyteller $ 9.95

Add $1.55 shipping/handling for each book   _____

Colorado residents add .45 tax   _____

      Total amount enclosed   _____

Name_____

Address_____

City/State/Zip_____

Phone_____

Create Your Own
STORYTELLING STORIES

Vivian Dubrovin
Illustrated By Bobbi Shupe

$12.95

4 issues
$9.95

STORYCRAFT
PUBLISHING
P.O. Box 205, Masonville CO 80541-0205